sear

341.5679

Why Can't Men Open Up?

Why Can't

Overcoming Men's Fear

Men

of Intimacy

Open Up?

By
Steven Naifeh and Gregory White Smith

Clarkson N. Potter, Inc./Publishers
DISTRIBUTED BY CROWN PUBLISHERS, INC. NEW YORK

Published by Clarkson N. Potter, Inc.,
One Park Avenue, New York, New York 10016 and simultaneously in Canada by General Publishing Company Limited

Manufactured in the United States of America

Grateful acknowledgment is hereby made to the following for permission to reprint excerpted materials in this book:

"Intimacy: Why It's So Crucial Today" by Michael Korda, copyright © 1981 by The Conde Nast Publications, Inc. Reprinted by permission of *Self* magazine.

Real Men Don't Eat Quiche by Bruce Feirstein, Text copyright © 1982 by Bruce Feirstein, Illustrations copyright © 1982 by Lee Lorenz. Reprinted by permission of Pocket Books, a division of Simon & Schuster, Inc.

Minor Characters by Joyce Johnson, copyright © 1983 by Joyce Johnson. Reprinted by permission of Houghton Mifflin Company.

The Neurotic Personality of Our Time by Karen Horney, M.D., copyright 1937 © renewed 1964 by W. W. Norton & Company, Inc. Reprinted by permission of W. W. Norton & Company, Inc.

Neurosis and Human Growth by Karen Horney, M.D., copyright 1950 © renewed 1978 by W. W. Norton & Company, Inc. Reprinted by permission of W. W. Norton & Company, Inc.

Library of Congress Cataloging in Publication Data

Naifeh, Steven W., 1952–
　　　Why can't men open up?

　　　1. Men—Psychology.　2. Interpersonal communication.
3. Intimacy (Psychology)　I. Smith, Gregory White.
II. Title.
HQ1090.N34　1984　　305.3'1　　83-24466
ISBN 0-517-54996-4
10 9 8 7 6 5 4 3 2 1
First Edition

for Connie Clausen

Contents

Acknowledgments

A good book, like a good relationship, is a collaborative effort. There may be only two names on the jacket, but there are hundreds of people between the covers. Even more than most authors, we have been favored with gifts of time, expertise, and insight for which we are eager to express our gratitude.

Because we are not members of the psychiatric community, we are especially indebted to the psychiatrists, psychologists, and therapists who helped us compensate for that deficiency by giving generously of ther expertise and experience. Dr. Ari Kiev, a prominent psychiatrist and author, was particularly generous with his time and wisdom. Dr. Alan A. Stone, who as a professor at Harvard had taught us to better understand ourselves, helped us to better understand the true nature of intimacy. In the field of psychohormonal research—a field filled with hawkers and hucksters—Dr. John Money at Johns Hopkins was a beacon of reason and scientific lucidity. Dr. Marilyn Machlowitz, an expert on psychology in the workplace, as well as a friend, read the manuscript in its earliest incarnations and pointed us to other experts. Although we never met him, we must give a special thanks to Dr. Joseph H. Pleck, whose compilation of research on the subject of masculinity is the inevitable basis for all further study in this area.

Among the other professionals who shared their insights with us, we should mention Dr. Hal Arkowitz, Tucson; Dr. Albert Ellis, New York; Richard Franklin, Minneapolis; Dr. Robert Garfield, Philadelphia; Dr. Helen Singer Kaplan, New York; Dr. Doreen Kimura, London, Ontario, Canada; Dr. Alexander Levay, New York; Cese MacDonald, New York and Westchester County; Marcha Ortiz, Washington, D.C.; Dr. David Peretz, New York; Dr. Virginia Sadock, New York; Dr. Alexander B. Taylor, Los Angeles; Dr. Josef H. Weissberg, New York; Dr. Robert Whitaker, Madison; Dr. Janet Wolfe, New York; and Dr. Judith Worrell, Louisville. Dr. Lewis Long of Alexandria, Virginia, and Dr. Maurizia Tovo of Nashville, Tennessee, read the manuscript carefully and provided detailed criticism.

Although he doesn't have any extra letters before or after his name to prove it, Tom Lynch of Roslyn, New York, is an expert in his own right and we want to thank him for his unique contribution to our understanding of the problem described in this book. For those who are tempted to belittle the importance or the difficulty of opening up, we recommend a conversation with Tom. In the same vein, a word of thanks is due to the Betty Friedans and Gloria Steinems of the men's liberation movement: Donald Bell, Warren Farrell, Marc Feigin Fasteau, Herb Goldberg, and Andrew Tolson. One of the surprises of this book was the hostility and ridicule heaped on the men's liberation movement by some women. We think the abuse is undeserved and self-indicting.

There are many others who lent credibility without credentials to the book. These are the 153 people who appear simply as "a woman in San Francisco" or "a man in Boston" or in some other anonymous form. We will resist the temptation to list their names here. They know who they are and they know that we are grateful.

Among the nonexperts who deserve a special mention are Pat Clements, Gary Fitts, Sarah Fitzsimmons, Joe Hartzler, Carolyn Naifeh, and Kathryn Smith—all of whom read the manuscript at various stages and shared with us unhesitantly both the smiles of their approval and the sting of their complaints. Service above and beyond the call of friendship was also rendered by Linda Chevalier, James K. Chiu and Dolores Hughes, Hume A. Horan, Andrea Kormann, Dan Ranger, and Christine Reynolds.

There are others who helped in various special ways to make this a better book: Jim Allen, John Anderson, Gordon Atkinson, Susan Bayley, Deborah Berger, Jeff Boss, Brad Brian, Dolores Brockmeyer, John Cahill, Andrew Cheney-Feid, Marc Chevalier, Lillian and Tjarda Claggett, Melanie Clements, William and Carolyn Cramer, William and Cynthia Dougherty, Richard de Combray, Malcolm Diamond, Amy Fitts, Wendy Gates, Brian Gilbert, Lisa Harms, Mark O. Haroldson, Bonnie Naifeh Hill, Susan Hunter, Pamela Hurt, Kyoko Ishikawa, Sally Kemp, Russ Kupfrian, Richard Kvam, Arline Lanphear, Martin N. Leaf, Suzanne Levine, Alice Long, Ann Luppi, Charles and Ellen Maneikis, Michael Morgenstern, Diane Acker Nygard, Patrick O'Connor, Leslie Palmer, Eileen Peretz, Roger Sherman, Claire Spiegel, Nancy Starr, Jamie Stobie, Patience Stoddard, William Strong, Terry Thompson, Suzanne Tichenor, Ann Vernon, Melissa von Stade, and the women's discussion group at the Orwell on Central Park West in New York City.

In any book of this nature, it is easy to veer off course on the road from conception to publication. If you're lucky, as we were, there is somebody nearby to point you back in the right direction. This was a particular problem here because we were trying to see a man's problem—our problem —from a woman's perspective. Among the many women who came to our rescue were Nancy Evans, Nicole Gregory, Margaret Jaworski, Eileen Herbert Jordan, Connie Leisure, and Susan Margolis. We owe a special debt of gratitude to Sherry Suib Cohen and Susan Edmiston, who led the search party and provided us with roadmaps. Without them, we never would have found our way to this point.

At Clarkson N. Potter we have received the kind of cooperation and support that is an author's most elusive reward. At various stages, we have incurred debts of gratitude to Ann Coleman, Gael Dillon, Susan Eilertsen, Laura Fagin, Michael Fragnito, Carolyn Hart, Nancy Kahan, Elizabeth Martin, Nancy Novograd, and Michelle Sidrane. No one has committed more time or care to the book than our editor, Carol Southern. She read each final manuscript as if it were the last and was patient and helpful to the end. Guy Kettelhack offered sage suggestions and much-needed encouragement. But finally it was Connie Clausen who managed somehow to make the process bearable and the result worth the effort. She is not only a rich vein of life experience and wisdom, she is a *femme extraordinaire* and the best argument for opening up we know.

SN
GWS

I'd learned myself by the age of sixteen that just as girls guarded their virginity, boys guarded something less tangible which they called Themselves. They seemed to believe they had a mission in life, from which they could easily be deflected by being exposed to too much emotion.

Joyce Johnson, *Minor Characters*

Part One:

Why Can't Men Open Up?

What Do Women Want?

"Sex, Schmex, Just Get Him to Talk to Me"

HY CAN'T MEN open up? It's a question that almost every woman in America has asked at some time in some way. Whether with a husband or a lover, almost every woman has felt the frustration of being emotionally shut out by a man she loves. It's as if a door closes and she's left outside in the cold.

Even when a woman knows a man loves her, she wonders why he can't say it. When something is bothering him, why can't he talk about it, share it, let her help him cope with it? Why is he afraid to show that he's vulnerable? Men taste pain, feel joy, shed tears, need love, suffer jealousy. Why must they do these things so often in silence and alone?

It's not easy for anyone, man or woman, to be emotionally open and honest in important relationships. The higher the stakes, the greater the risk of being hurt. But why are men, as a rule, less willing to take that risk? Certainly the sixties and seventies have had an impact. Consciousness-raising, assertiveness training, encounter groups, the "me" generation, and "getting in touch with yourself" have filtered through to some men. Yet many of these changes, it seems, have been only temporary adaptations, "pseudo" changes, cut to suit the fashion of the times. Now the times are changing again and the fashion seems to be returning to "real men" with the "right stuff." The result: many men are still imprisoned in emotional isolation, living out repressive masculine roles.

Even though many men today have a clearer awareness of their need for emotional fulfillment, the essence of what it means to "be a man" has changed surprisingly little. The pillars of maleness continue to be strength, invulnerability, and maintaining a competitive edge. Many men continue to feel that they must prove themselves every day. For many men, even after years of changing stereotypes, emotional honesty and openness are still among the sacrifices they must make to manhood.

The result, especially in marriages, is hurt, misunderstanding, and anger. In *Medical Aspects of Human Sexuality*, four hundred leading psychiatrists were asked why marriages fail. Forty-five percent of them said that the primary cause of divorce in America was the husband's inability to communicate his feelings. Only 9 percent blamed sexual incompatibility. In a survey of a thousand people, Dr. Michael McGill, author of *Changing Him, Changing Her*, found that the change women want most is for men to talk about their feelings, and the change men want most is to be understood without having to talk about their feelings.

Women feel that they're being locked out of men's emotional lives. They complain that men want them only for sex and housekeeping, not for love or friendship. They feel that they're forced to turn to other women for the care and concern of true friendship. For these women, men may offer physical intimacy and sexual fulfillment, but not emotional intimacy or personal fulfillment. They're left, in the words of one frustrated wife, "standing at the gates, alternately trying to pry them open and banging to get in."

Some men feel threatened, confused, and assaulted by women's demands for honesty and openness, for some kind of fluent emotional exhange. After all, these are demands that earlier generations of women never made. The old formulas for male-female relationships that made life easier, if not more fulfilling, are no longer enough—nor are they sanctioned any longer by the culture. In a world of changing values, men are facing more demands for intimacy than ever before. It's an unsettling time to be a man.

Why can't men open up? That question, bursting with frustration and exasperation, was first thrown at us during a women's discussion-group meeting we attended as part of the research for a book on sexual relationships. Expecting to catch some choice inside tips on how women like to have men make love, we found instead that making love was not really on their minds.

In a grand old apartment building on Central Park West, the discussion group met regularly to explore issues of common concern. Despite their sharp-eyed skepticism, they allowed us to sit in. They were mostly working women: attractive, well put together, ambitious, and articulate—so articulate that we soon felt uncomfortable. They were hitting too close to home, framing our problems, men's problems. In only two hours of discussion, we learned more about how women see men than we had learned in a lifetime of growing up male in America.

Jennifer, who hosted the meeting, told us, "Speaking for myself, when things are going well in my relationship with my husband, the sex is good. When they're not, the sex is awful. It's as simple as that." The other women nodded and murmured in agreement. Then she said, "The *relationship* is everything. My husband doesn't need a book on how to make love. He needs a book on how to make a relationship. How to say 'I love you,' how to open up and let me into his life."

There was a commotion of agreement. "That's right," came a voice from somewhere in the back. "Sex, schmex. Just get him to talk to me." That comment was the seed from which this book sprang. It was the starting point for our investigation into men's fear of intimacy and the pall it casts on their relationships with women.

When women plead, "Just get him to talk to me," they don't simply want to trade pronouncements; they want much more. Just as there is more to love than "I love you," there is more to intimacy than conversation. A man can hide behind a veil of words, of masculine jocularity and glibness, as easily as behind a wall of silence.

For these women, *talking* meant the whole, complex process by which a person shares a part of himself or herself with another: breaking through the wall of everyday chatter and making a genuine connection. It can happen with or without warning, with or without words: talking quietly in bed or shouting over the dinnertime din; looking up from the morning paper or the evening dishes, just sharing a comfortable silence.

But such moments of deep connection are all too rare, especially in ongoing relationships, where the anxious efforts of courtship often give way to familiarity and indifference. The more we talked to women, the more clearly the message came through: "Sex, schmex, just get him to talk to me."

The same message, amplified thousands of times, can be heard in a survey conducted by the *Ladies' Home Journal* in January 1983. In contrast to earlier surveys, the *Journal* found that 82 percent of the 83,000 respondents felt that their sexual relationships were "satisfying." Almost half said they made love three to five times a week. The problem for unhappy wives lay elsewhere. "The most important factor in a happy, sexy marriage," the survey reported, ". . . is the ability of both husband and wife to express their feelings. . . . When we looked at what distinguished the happy wives in our survey from the unhappy wives, it was the frequency of expressing love verbally which turned out to be one of the most significant factors."

As we researched this book, we saw in living detail the

problems are same men are women we need to work together on the problems instead of constantly complaining

problem that Jennifer and millions of women like her confront every day: men who refuse to talk, men who resist intimacy, men who are emotionally isolated and unable to ask for help. For the first time, we saw men as many women do.

We also saw ourselves. At first, it was easy to think that Jennifer's accusing finger was pointed at men in general, not at us as individuals. We started our research in that spirit —pursuing other people's stories of emotional isolation, other men's inability to communicate; trying to understand why *Men* can't open up.

But the truth would home to roost. Our decision to deal with the problem from the safety of the journalistic third person was the most convincing proof of Jennifer's point. It was the smoking pistol, and we were holding it. Keeping emotional distance was so much a part of our lives that understanding of our own involvement was a long, hard time in coming.

But gradually we realized that the "problem of intimacy" had always been there in our lives; we had just refused to notice. It was there when a high-school girl friend wanted to "just sit and talk." It was there when a woman wanted to hear "those three little words" before going to bed. It was there when no male friends showed up in a crunch. It was there when the heart ached with love but the mouth would hardly budge.

As fully grown adults, we looked at ourselves in the mirror for the first time. We saw the reflections of men, but they were hardly recognizable. This book is an effort to describe those images in the glass. It's a group portrait, and we all must take our places in it.

Does the Rock Talk to the Wave?

Why can't men open up? Why do men insist on keeping an emotional distance while women plead for intimacy and support? How different are the emotional needs of men and women?

It is possible to overstate the differences, certainly. Not all women are open, nor are all men closed. Yet men and women, in general, do have different ways of expressing their emotional needs. Where many men try to guard their feelings or deny them, many women share them eagerly; where many men tend to hold themselves at a safe distance from the emotions of others, many women tend to give emotional support as readily as they accept it. To feel truly fulfilled, a person must both give and receive, and many men are equipped to do neither. "In affairs of the heart," one psychologist told us, "men and women often speak different languages."

"Our house was on a long, isolated stretch of beach," said Judy, a handsome woman with sun-bleached hair who, at thirty-five, had just divorced her husband of ten years. "The water was so close you could hear the waves breaking against the rocks all day and all night. Wave after wave after wave. I used to think how we were like that, Tom and me. There I was, constantly washing up against Tom, but never getting anywhere. I was the wave, he was the rock. Does the rock talk to the wave? I suppose if I could have kept it up for centuries I might have been able to wear him down a little."

Men and women are often as different emotionally as the rock and the wave. Most people think a man is supposed to be competitive, aggressive, thick-skinned, and goal-oriented. He is a rock of strength and independence, unmoved by the flow of emotions around him. He is, in Ernest Hemingway's phrase, an "island in the stream." A woman, on the other hand, often shapes herself to suit her environment. She is accommodating and receptive, not unmoved or unmoving. She becomes a part of what she meets, interacting, taking, returning, responding.

Dr. Virginia Sadock, a New York psychiatrist, says: "Men usually fight for what they want with more force than women. When you're a woman, you generally grow up attuned to other people's thinking. Are you pleasing the people around you? That's the way you tend to get what you want. Women are more sensitive to another person's approving look, or disapproving look. Men will just plow ahead."

When these two emotional opposites meet—when a closed man and an open woman come together—it's not surprising that they often fail to forge a connection through which can pass the intimacy they both long for.

Opening Up

Although men and women express their emotional needs differently, the needs themselves are the same. Ultimately, a man's struggle to open up is a human struggle: part of the broader struggle shared by every individual, man or woman, for genuine emotional sharing. This kind of sharing doesn't come easily. It has to be preceded by a degree of self-awareness and emotional self-fulfillment. Before people can "reach out and touch someone" they first have to reach inside and touch themselves.

According to the psychiatrist Karen Horney, every person, man or woman, has a "real self," a "central inner force common to all human beings and yet unique to each, which is the deep source of growth." A healthy individual, says Horney, is one who can "develop the unique alive forces of his real self: the clarity and depth of his own feelings, thoughts, wishes, interests; the ability to tap his own resources, the strength of his will power; the special capabilities or gifts he may have; the faculty to express himself and to relate himself to others with his spontaneous feelings."

Horney's description of what happens when a person loses touch with this "real self" applies to both sexes, but it echoes with disturbing clarity what many women told us about the men in their lives. "His feelings," says Horney, "seem to have lost their intensity and are dulled and flattened out. . . . It is as if he had shut away his real self in a sound-proof room." The result is "a general impoverishment of [his] emotional life showing in a diminished sincerity, spontaneity, and depth of feelings, or at least in a restricted range of possible feelings."

In this emotional aridity, a closed man's behavior is inevitably controlled by stereotypes and expectations. In Horney's words, a man "molds himself into something he is not. He feels what he *should* feel, wishes what he *should* wish, likes what he *should* like. In other words, the tyranny of the should drives him frantically to be something other than what he is or could be. And in his imagination he *is* different—so different, indeed, that his real self fades and pales still more."

Opening up is the process of bringing a man's real self and his outer self back together, or reconnecting a man's actions to his feelings, of giving them intensity and full color. Expressions of affection and love that would seem easy, come hard to many men. "I can sit here and say, 'I love my wife,' or 'I love my kids,'" one man told us, "and that's a major victory by itself. Most of my life I couldn't have done that."

The open man is a free man. Because his actions are connected to his impulses, he can be spontaneous. Because he's no longer protecting his feelings from the people who could hurt them, he's vulnerable. The open man is warm, in the sense that the hot core of his emotions, desires, and dreams is always just beneath the surface of his daily life. He is, in the words of Tom Lynch, who leads a male encounter group in Roslyn, Long Island, "up front" about what makes him happy and what gives him pain. He has "a greater sense of himself, a sharpened sense of direction."

The "openness" of the open man is akin to an attitude toward life that Karen Horney called "wholeheartedness"—an ability "to be without pretense, to be emotionally sincere, to be able to put the whole of oneself into one's feelings, one's work, one's beliefs."

But there's more to true openness than emotional spontaneity. "The will to express your feelings," says Dr. Alan Stone, professor of law and psychiatry at Harvard Law School and Harvard Medical School, "is an important part of communication. But it's important to distinguish between self-indulgent expressions of feeling that are meant to manipulate the other person and a responsible sharing of your feelings.

"A narcissistic expression of feelings," Dr. Stone told us, "can be the basis of emotional blackmail, bullying, and whining, and all sorts of vices, in the old-fashioned sense of the word. Narcissistic expressions of feelings were typical of the 'me' generation, a part of self-actualization and the human potential movement. People were encouraged to communicate their feelings as they felt them, as if they were in a therapeutic not a human relationship.

"The result was a great deal of confusion between genuine emotional sharing between people who care about each other and simply telling your troubles in a self-centered way. In any close relationship there is a certain amount of listening to troubles and comforting a partner. I worry that this tends to be all that 'being open about your feelings' means to many people.

"In opening up, a man must not only fulfill his own need for catharsis, but also the other person's need for empathy. He has a need to be cared about, she has a need to care. Without an awareness of the other person's needs, a man who thinks he's opening up is really just talking to himself. Opening up becomes an exercise in narcissism, like primping in a mirror.

"The reason for encouraging men to share their feelings —the goal—is to increase the possibility for intimacy. Telling somebody your problems is a part of intimacy, but not all of it. Intimacy requires reciprocity."

The Child Inside

As a man grows up and develops an adult personality, he builds up layers of control and repression. He's taught to deny his emotions, or at least translate them into the language of manhood. If he integrates these lessons into his life, he becomes closed. At the extreme, protecting his sense of his own manhood can become more important to him than developing close personal relationships. Love for a woman becomes sexual domination. Love for another man becomes a handshake or a slap on the back. Love for a child becomes a strong disciplinary hand.

Much is lost in these translations. Sometimes our feelings are turned on their heads. Too many men can express tenderness only by toughness. Because the language of manhood allows us only a small range in which to express our emotions, it's hardly surprising that those emotions become distorted.

To open up is, first, to strip away those layers of control and repression that hide the core of innocence, authenticity, and spontaneity in every man. It is to forget the language of manhood and become fluent again in the language of emotion. Many men are condemned to walk through adult life in a heavy costume called "being a man." To be open, to be emotionally fulfilled, they need to reestablish contact with the child inside. They need to take off that costume and feel free again to smile, to cry, to touch and be touched.

Men *can* open up. There are no easy solutions, no foolproof formulas. In a man's struggle to discover emotional intimacy, he needs a woman's help. Each man, each woman, each relationship is a unique set of hopes, frustrations, promises, limitations, and joys. For that reason, we've peopled this book with men and women who have worked to create intimacy in their relationships; men and women whose stories are proof that the fear of intimacy, the fear that isolates so many men, can be overcome.

Confessions of Two Closed Men

THESE ARE NOT "confessions" in the sensational sense; there are no front-page scandals or dark secrets revealed. But for closed men, even the tamest self-revelation is an intimidating experience. These confessions consist only of random episodes from our pasts pieced together in an effort to capture a little of what it means to be a man in this society—brief introductory portraits to give the flavor of "manhood" and how it developed in two separate and very different lives.

We admit up front that we're not scholars or scientists; we're two men who, like millions of others, are trying to understand why we are the way we are. You might call these "notes from the other side of the wall." Our stories, we think, are not unusual. There are many men out there who would tell similar stories—if they would open up enough to let them out.

We begin with the familiar notion that men have it better. Although it's true that men enjoy certain privileges and reap the benefits of cultural favoritism, such advantages don't come cheap. What we gain in earning power, we often pay for in emotional repression and alienation—to say nothing of heart attacks and early death. "Although women are handicapped in achievement-oriented spheres," says Dr. Barbara Lusk Forisha, head of the behavioral sciences department at the University of Michigan, "men are handicapped in emotional spheres. Both sexes are deprived by the confines of their sex roles."

Through boyhood and adolescence, we pursued "manhood" with single-minded, almost manic determination. Not that we knew what "manhood" *was*. All we knew was that we waged furious little wars on our elephantine insecurities in the locker room, on the playing fields, and in relationships with women.

In this struggle, we were given numerous miscues by friends and foes alike. We were told, for example, that boys don't cry. So we obediently held back our tears of pain in order to earn from our fathers that highest of accolades: "What a big boy you are. You didn't cry." We didn't realize at the time, of course, what such accolades might eventually cost us.

From childhood, our lives took different roads. One of us grew up in a Midwestern environment of football, summer camp, junior proms, and "Can I have the keys to the car tonight, Dad?" The other was a Foreign Service brat, raised in a series of Third World posts by parents who worked for the U.S. State Department. Yet, despite our experiences on opposite sides of the world, we find our emotional pasts— and presents—strikingly similar. Facing the possibility of intimacy, we share with most men the same unexplored fears.

Greg: Scoring Goals. I remember most vividly the games we played when I was growing up. My brother and I played them with a ferociousness that seems, in retrospect, wildly out of proportion to their importance. Even at that early age, men learn to take themselves very seriously.

We bottled fireflies (the one with the most fireflies won), earned merit badges, and battled for control of the neighborhood. While my sister was having tea parties and talking to her dolls in funny voices, I was fighting crab-apple wars. We split into two teams and threw the hard little red grenades (the trees were laden with ammunition) until all the members of the other team were "dead."

I'm told that boys' play and girls' play have changed in the last thirty years, but when my sister and I were growing up, our games were usually different, and they taught us different lessons. The purpose of my games was to score. If someone suggested that we "just volley," there was always a round of derisive laughter: "Why don't you go play with the girls." I had fun, but fun wasn't the point. The *point* was the point.

The difference, of course, meant nothing to me at the time. I wasn't even dimly aware that there was something significant missing from my experiences, that my sister was developing both the emotional fluency necessary to express her feelings and the habit of intimacy with others, that I was growing up unschooled in the language of emotions and unprepared for the demands of intimacy. Later, when I crossed the threshold of a relationship for the first time, I entered a world almost completely unknown. But the women I met, like my sister, had been there before.

I'm sure the media—especially television—also played a key role in making me the kind of person I am. I followed TV westerns with the fanaticism of a Shiite martyr: the Lone Ranger, Matt Dillon, the Rifleman, Bronco Lane, Bret and Bart Maverick, the Cartwrights, and on and on. I was particularly devoted to the Roy Rogers show, at seven on Sunday evenings. I think back on that show, which riveted my young attention, and I recall that the most profound emotional attachments were between Roy and his horse, Trigger, and between Pat Brady and his jeep, Nellie Belle. Needless to say, Roy and Dale never talked over their emotional problems.

Later, in high school, I had a series of awkward relationships with girls, but an extremely satisfying and reciprocal relationship with my secondhand Chevelle Super Sport. Like many boys, I shared something special with my car. It represented independence, masculinity, adulthood, potency. Even as I struggled unsuccessfully to figure out the meaning of love, I lavished on my car a lover's care and attentiveness. Real men can't share their emotions, but they sure know how to treat their means of transportation. That was part of what I learned from Roy.

In adolescence, there were new demands. In sports, especially football (for which I had an irrational love), I learned that hardship should be savored, that pain is good for me, and that competition is man's highest achievement. But, as usual, I wasn't aware of the real lessons I was being taught. Like every defensive player on my football team, I wanted to play the position of "roverback" because he was free to roam the field; he wasn't keyed to any offensive player; he could pick his own man. He was as close as we could come to our Wild West cowboy fantasies. If only we could spend our whole lives as roverbacks. At the time, none of us saw any irony in the fact that the roverback was also called the "monster man."

What is the result of this meandering, potholed path to manhood? What has become of the kid from the crab-apple wars? Like most men, I'm someone who has trouble admitting he's wrong; I'm still looking for the "right" woman, dodging the possibility that I'm still not the right man. Like most men, I'm someone who needs love but, even today, chokes on that admission. For every time I've said "I love you," I must have said "I love you too" a hundred times. I'm someone whose brother died a decade ago, but has yet to shed a tear. Where are the accolades now?

Steve: The Lone Scout. Ever since I was a kid, I was expected to be on my own, to entertain myself. In Libya, one of my father's overseas posts, I had no choice. There were no other foreign children to play with, and the Libyan children were forbidden to play with us by their xenophobic parents.

A month after our arrival, a knot of dark-eyed little girls began to peer inquisitively at my sister from the safety of their walled villas. My sister peered back. After another month, the girls made a show of skipping rope. It was an invitation, and my sister accepted.

Meanwhile, to compensate for my lost adolescence, my father applied to the Boy Scouts of America to charter a Lone Scout Troop—the kind originally designed for isolated farm boys back in the U.S. Our application was granted, and we became the Boy Scouts of America, Lone Scout Troop, Baida, Libya, with my father as scoutmaster and me as the lone scout. For the next two years, while my sister skipped rope and played dolls with the Libyan girls on our street, I earned merit badges and hiked in the desert.

Baida was a beautiful city, set in the green hills of the North African coast, overlooking the supernaturally blue Mediterranean Sea. But since I was the only adolescent male among the handful of foreigners in Baida, the only language I learned was the language of my parents' social life—the language of cocktail parties, bridge games, and diplomatic receptions. I knew something of sex (in the mysterious ways that all kids do), and nothing of sports, but a great deal about North African politics, oil prices, and the need to maintain U.S. bases in Libya.

It was in that sad state of ignorance that, at age fourteen, I arrived at a boarding school in Delaware called St. Andrew's and found myself suddenly surrounded by a sea of adolescent males, all of them babbling about matters totally unfamiliar to me. Instead of politics, the international economy, and American defense, they talked about only two things: would St. Andrew's have another winning football season, and who had already "done it."

The topics seemed of inexhaustible interest to my fellow inmates in that somnambulant little community in the middle of Delaware chicken-farm country. For four years, the topic of conversation varied only slightly. Senior year, we talked briefly about getting into college and who got into where. But, inevitably, the conversation returned to the only topics of truly undying importance: would St. Andrew's have another winning football season, and who had already "done it."

The question, significantly, was *who* had done it, not *why* they had done it. The emphasis was entirely on the act itself, not on the context that might have made it meaningful. Because St. Andrew's was still all-male, dances were scheduled periodically with sister schools like Madeira and St. Timothy's. I can only guess at what the girls thought about those two frenzied hours of compulsory social contact, but for us they were as much a sport as football or rowing.

Some were better competitors than others, of course. The best in my class, the undisputed champion, was a boy with the Dickensian name of Bill Strong. Everyone in the school envied his way with women, his confidence, his reputation for sexual success.

Once, a week before the big spring dance, a time when the very word *zit* struck terror into more fragile hearts, Bill Strong stood up in the dining hall and drank a glassful of Hershey's chocolate syrup. It was an act of sheer unbridled confidence. That memorable day in the dining hall, no one doubted that Bill Strong was *numero uno,* a true champion in the great game of sex. We all stood and cheered our admiration and envy.

After the dance was over, another boy went around the school filling out a chart he had devised. You received a certain number of points for touching a certain part of a girl's anatomy, a certain number of points for a kiss, etc. Needless to say, there was no place on his chart for "successfully sharing emotional intimacy."

I arrived at college prepared for romance only as a competitive sport. So, instead of facing the unknown world of emotions, I retreated into the more familiar world of work. I told myself that I would put off my emotional life long enough to do well at school, so I spent my days writing essays on topics like "Wordsworth and Loneliness" as I gazed out the library windows with repressed envy at couples playing Frisbee on the lawn. In law school, I entered several relationships, but I was never willing to commit the investment of time and attention necessary to make any of them really fulfilling.

Then, finally, I let myself fall in love—*really* in love. That certainly wasn't a cure for my work mania, but it did put my problems in boldface. It forced me to confront the fact that I had become a certifiable workaholic with no experience and no skill in the world of emotions. I was hiding behind a wall of activity. The familiar routine of hard work had become preferable to the unknown challenges of intimacy. I was afraid to test myself, to make myself vulnerable in a personal relationship.

One night last fall, when I returned to my apartment after a sixteen-hour day of interviewing, there was a message on my telephone answering machine from the woman I loved. She wanted me to go to the new Woody Allen film with her. But I had deadlines to meet and knew that I would have to work all night to meet them. So I didn't call her right away. I didn't call her the next day. In fact, I didn't call her for several days, and by the time I did, the relationship had been fatally wounded. At the time, I justified my behavior as fulfilling my duty, advancing my career, keeping my priorities straight. Now I know that just the opposite was true; my priorities were all wrong. Now I realize that the longer I shy away from intimacy, the harder it will be for me to accept the risks of reaching for it. However daunting those risks may be, they're nothing compared to the risks of not trying.

These are the rough outlines of our stories. The details may be different, but the theme is the same. We were raised to be closed men. The lessons we learned—at the dinner table, in the locker room, in front of the television set— were lessons in avoiding intimacy. By closing ourselves off to feelings, we thought we could escape the anxieties and disappointments of emotional involvement. We've discovered since, sometimes painfully, that we were wrong.

Some men escape this fate. Just as there are closed women, there are open men—men who for many reasons missed the indoctrination that we underwent. The culture that made it difficult for us to express our feelings may be changing, but there are still too many men like us who mortgaged their manhoods and assumed the burdens of emotional reticence in exchange for the most superficial tokens of masculinity.

In the course of researching this book, we spoke with hundreds of men who had come to realize that something was missing from their lives. The stories these men told us, like our own stories, often had an uplifting side in which a woman played a crucial role. We also spoke to the women who lived with these men and helped them better understand why they were closed and what they could do to change. Finally, we interviewed dozens of experts—psychologists, psychiatrists, and therapists—who have devoted their lives to helping men overcome their fear of dependency.

In the end, we discovered that despite the unseen causes and historical handicaps, most closed men are looking for a better way to live their lives, to share intimacy, to confront their emotions, and to express their love.

Why can't men open up? The answer is here: they can.

Fears of Falling

**How the Culture of Manhood Works
Against Intimacy**

UE LARGELY TO the women's movement, closed men—all men—have undergone some important changes. For example, the modern closed man may do his part to keep a household running, help care for the baby, or report to a female boss. These and other changes represent a significant movement away from the traditional "strong, silent man." But those older cultural stereotypes can still emerge when it comes time for a man to say, "I need you," or to share his emotional life as well as the chores.

Men's hearts may be the last frontier for the women's movement. "We can overcome stereotypes that keep women down economically, politically, and socially," says an editor at a prominent women's magazine, "but if we can't overcome the emotional stereotypes that keep men from being able to relate to women, all we'll have is half a loaf. What I want for myself is what I think most women want, a rewarding professional life and a rewarding personal life. If that means setting men free—and I think it does—then we should work just as hard at that as we do for equal opportunity."

＊ The men most dramatically affected by cultural changes

in the last decade, according to experts, are highly educated men, men in the professions rather than in business, and men in fields that have admitted large numbers of women. "My generation is just different," says a twenty-eight-year-old woman in Milwaukee. "A lot of women I know are married to open men, men they can laugh with, men who help with the chores, men who are really their friends."

But Dr. Alexander B. Taylor, a therapist in Beverly Hills, cautions: "Some young men seem to open up because they know they're supposed to open up, not because they feel it. It's a kind of pseudo-openness. They play the game of 'more authentic than thou.' Really opening up is a profoundly thoughtful and feeling process." It will be some time, of course, before we can assess the permanence of recent changes, before we will know whether this generation is really different, if their relationships are really more open and reciprocal than those of their parents.

"Traditionally," says Harvard's Dr. Alan Stone, "women are pushed in the direction of developing their inner selves because they weren't allowed to develop their outer selves. Men, on the other hand, were so determined to develop their outer selves—their achieving, doing, acting sides —that the development of an inner self was always considered effeminate. But I think the stereotypes are changing."

In other words, men and women are hammering at the same wall, but from opposite sides. As women are struggling to break out of the limitations of dependency, men are struggling to break in. As women are exploring the outer world of self-sufficiency, men are coming back to the inner world of intimacy. This process of sharing each other's worlds creates new problems as well as new possibilities. Fighting for their independence, many women fall prey to the same fear of intimacy that has plagued men. Yet the possibilities for self-discovery, for coming together, and for deeper understanding are better than they've ever been.

Dr. Robert Garfield, professor of psychiatry at Hahnemann Medical College in Philadelphia, says, "The struggle of the eighties for women is the struggle for individuation. Women are saying, what can I ask of myself, what can I claim for myself, who am I? For men, the struggle of the eighties is the struggle for intimacy: What can I accept for myself, what can I give to others, who am I?"

How Men Are Different

As Drs. Stone and Garfield suggest, some of the problems men face in overcoming their fear of intimacy are the result of deep divisions in the society. Women traditionally have been expected to raise children, maintain the family unit, and sustain the community's emotional life. Men, as our own stories illustrate, are brought up to do business in the community and provide for their families. To fill this role more successfully, young men are trained in certain strengths, skills, and attitudes.

There may also be deeper, prior ways in which manhood works against intimacy. Recently, researchers have begun to discover the different ways in which male and female brains develop in the womb. Their preliminary and still controversial findings are that the left side of the brain, which controls verbal and cognitive skills, develops more rapidly in little girls than in little boys. There is also evidence that the right brain, which controls visual and spatial functions, develops more fully in boys. The result, as most mothers and kindergarten teachers know, is that little boys are less verbal than their female schoolmates. The physiological difference will eventually disappear, but during these early formative years, boys often develop insecurity in verbal interaction and retreat to the world of hand-eye games and visual interaction in which their better developed right brains give them the advantage. This insecurity often persists into adulthood. Just as little boys tend to prefer math and gym while little girls favor reading and writing, big boys tend to ogle pictures in *Playboy* for sexual stimulation while big girls indulge in romance novels.

Whatever their predispositions, it is mainly through

games and play that children learn their cultural lessons. The writer Julius Lester remembers how it was for him, growing up: ". . . the girls sitting in the shade of porches, playing with their dolls, toy refrigerators, and stoves. There was the life, I thought! No constant pressure to prove oneself. No necessity always to be competing. While I humiliated myself on the football and baseball fields, the girls stood on the sidelines laughing at me, because they didn't have to do anything except be girls. The rising of each sun brought me to the starting line of yet another day's Olympic decathlon, with no hope of ever winning even a bronze medal. . . . [Girls] didn't have to do anything except be girls."

This boyhood training, which combines equal parts of exhortation and humiliation, develops a very special kind of man: goal-oriented, competitive, in control, and independent. In short, the inexpressive, closed man. Of course, not every man is all of these things. And no man, we hope, conforms in every detail to the model we describe here. But there is a little of the closed man inside most of us. Whether it takes the form of competitiveness, an obsession with goals, a need to be in control, or an urge to independence, that part of the closed man in each of us is making it harder for us to enjoy real intimacy.

Competitive and Goal-Oriented. Most men are conditioned from childhood to be goal-oriented; they find out early that "the point is the point." But part of being intimate is enjoying each other's company, wanting to be with someone not because you have some business to transact or some goal to achieve, but because you take pleasure in a quiet exchange of observations, ideas, and emotions. That kind of free-flowing conversation is almost unknown to men, who are raised to believe that every minute of the day must be "productive," that everything they do must have some immediate purpose.

"Most men need reasons for everything," a woman in Portland, Maine, told us. "Every time they see somebody, it has to be hung on an event, there's got to be a reason. They have to be *doing* something together. *Being* together isn't enough. So they have trouble developing the kind of emotional bond I think women develop, the kind of bond where you can talk about everything from your innermost fears and hopes to how much you paid for bacon." A man, of course, is not supposed to talk about bacon; he's just supposed to bring it home.

"Did you ever notice," asked a woman in Boston named Bonnie, "how when a man calls a male friend up for lunch, his friend will say something like 'What's up?', 'What's the story?', or 'What can I do for you?' But when a woman calls a female friend up for lunch, her friend will say, 'Sure,' or just 'When?' " Women are accustomed to meeting simply to enjoy each other's company, a pleasure and a luxury many men may feel has been forbidden to them.

For most women, conversation has always been a crucial part of emotional life, engaged in for its own sake, its purpose not so much to exchange some specific information as to keep the lines of communication open and active. "Feelings are the bones of a relationship," says a woman dress designer in Los Angeles, "but it's the words that flesh it out."

The ultimate failure of the closed man's conversation is that it doesn't appreciate the value of small talk, of emotional "trivia." In human relationships, very little is really trivial. The importance of any fact depends on the context of caring. In a loving relationship, the irrelevant or insignificant is the cement that binds a couple together, providing a continuum of feelings that makes intimacy possible. When a man dismisses "trivial" conversation, which may be silly, playful, and probably without clear objectives, he's also rejecting the very intimacy he craves.

In relationships, as in game-playing, men need a goal to give their efforts shape and meaning. Thus, the emphasis on conquest among young men. Responding to the challenge of a goal, a man can summon up whatever is required to achieve that goal—even a sort of emotional honesty. But once the prize is won, once the woman says yes, once the relationship is consummated (sexually, emotionally, or maritally), problems begin. All too often, because there is no longer any clearly defined goal, a man's interest wanes, and with it his desire. The *arrangement* often continues—from need, convenience, or simple familiarity—but his heart isn't in it.

The closed man's inability to function without goals extends even to lovemaking. In sex, the goal is simple: orgasm. A respondent in the *Hite Report* registered the common male perception that men pursue intercourse not for biological or emotional reasons but because they are "brought up to feel that a vital part of being a man" is the sex act itself.

The goal is not entirely self-centered; women do play a part in the game. But for some men it *is* a game, as much as dodge ball or marbles. Many men "don't approach lovemaking as participants out to share an enjoyable experience," according to Dr. Mary Calderone, the noted sex educator; "they're *performers,* forced to prove to themselves that they are very, very good. They want—they *need*—victory, gold stars, the genuine applause and response of their audience of one. Their partner's orgasm is the sexual gold medal they are after and the key to their own sexual self-acceptance."

Not just sex, but all physical contact between men and women suffers. For the closed man, almost every contact must have a purpose. Women complain routinely that men don't know how to touch or hug, to cuddle or caress without wanting to proceed immediately to intercourse.

"When a woman wishes to be cuddled and nothing more," says Dr. Marc H. Hollender, chairman of the department of psychiatry at Vanderbilt University School of Medicine, "her message may be, and often is, misunderstood by her partner. She separates her desire to be held from her wish for sexual activity. When a man responds sexually to the woman who only wants to be held, she feels put upon. When the woman rebuffs the man's advances, he feels she has misled him. Clearly, there are crossed wires in the communication system."

If goal-orientation can be harmful to a relationship, competition can be deadly. A childhood of games and gamesmanship teaches a boy to see every challenge in life as a competition. "Winning isn't everything; it's the only thing." It's no accident that sports and war have often captured men's imaginations and that their terminology so often dominates men's conversations.

Of course, the last ten years have shown that women can be just as competitive as men, on the playing field and in the job market. What really distinguishes men from women is not their capacity for competitiveness, but their choice of playing fields. If most women will compete when the stakes are right, many men will compete for the sport of it, baring their competitive teeth even on the most noncompetitive—and inappropriate—occasions.

"From the time we wake up in the morning," a housewife in Lincoln, Nebraska, told us, "he has to be superior. He tells me that he got up earlier, and that makes him a better person. Or he jogs more regularly. Or he plans more of the vacation. Everything is a contest. He can't even play a game with the kids without trying to win." Raised from childhood to be competitive, even in lovemaking and child rearing, a man has less chance to develop the kind of mutual respect and trust that are crucial to intimate relationships.

Independent and in Control. "American westerns were never about the American West," a female television producer in Los Angeles explained to us. "They were about American manhood. The stories are always about this one man pitted against the elements, the Indians, or the bad guys. If there's a woman at all, she's usually killed at the beginning so the hero can go out and face his destiny. No one would believe this guy would risk his life if his wife is waiting offscreen. A man with a wife and family makes compromises; a man without them can afford to accept the impossible challenge, fight the good fight. To really be a man, the American cowboy had to be alone."

The need to stand alone affects all men's lives, from

their relationships with others to their attitude toward work. In order to be truly independent, a man must reject any demands from those close to him. Independence is like loyalty, a male executive told the *Harvard Business Review*— it's not an on-again, off-again thing. "You can't express dependence when you feel it," he said, "because it's a kind of absolute. If you are loyal ninety percent of the time and disloyal ten percent, would you be considered loyal? Well, the same happens with dependence; you are either dependent or independent; you can't be both."

This uncompromising insistence on independence often means that a man resents having any demands placed on him at all. He resists telling his wife where he's going. He is upset when she accepts an invitation on his behalf. He resists giving affection when it's asked for. After all, a man can't permit others to assume a position of control in his life, either physical or emotional. If he allows himself emotional intimacy with a woman, it must be on a "no demands" basis; to respond to demands is to acknowledge a loss of control and independence. Therefore, he finds it easier to support a woman if she doesn't demand support; to give love if she doesn't request it; to answer if she doesn't ask.

In order to maintain emotional independence, a closed man controls his emotions; he doesn't allow his emotions to control him. He may feel pain—physical or emotional—but he doesn't let that raw feeling out. He absorbs it, refines it, and shows the world only what he chooses to. "The more something affects my boyfriend emotionally," a young woman in Kansas City complained to us, "the less he shows it. He cried when the [Kansas City] Chiefs lost the Super Bowl, but he couldn't shed a tear when his father died. That would have been admitting too much."

Hurting, both physical and emotional, is part of manhood. Even in the high-school years and earlier, boys are pushed into competition that makes injury likely and pain inevitable. During the last decade, there have been repeated outcries about high-school, junior-high, and even elementary-school sports programs in which both coaches and parents minimize the significance of physical suffering and create a climate in which injured players are anesthetized and sent back into a game, often resulting in permanent physical disabilities. All of this in the obsessive pursuit of a winning season.

Just as a man is cheered for suppressing his feelings—for gritting his teeth and bearing it—he's condemned for allowing feelings to show. When Edmund Muskie stood in the New Hampshire snow and made a moving defense of his wife against some campaign slander and declared his love for her, there were tears in his eyes. Those tears, most political analysts believe, cost Muskie the Democratic nomination for president in 1972. Said one commentator at the time: "Do we want a man who cries to sit down and bargain with the Russians?"

"If I want to cry at a movie, I cry at a movie," says an unmarried Boston woman in her thirties. "Somewhere along the line, probably in the crib, I must have learned that it was okay to cry. A man, on the other hand, is allowed to weep only if his entire family has been killed. If his city is in ruins and everyone he ever loved is dead, maybe he can shed a few tears. I don't think men are born without a capacity to express their emotions. I just think it's been socialized out of them."

"I'd never seen my husband cry," a Chicago woman in her late forties told us, "through hard economic times, the death of both his parents, a long illness, until our son died in an accident. Then he just fell apart. At the funeral, every time a friend of our son's came up to him, he burst into tears. He'd been such a rock all those years, and suddenly it just melted away." On the rare occasions when men admit to having cried, they often use the telling circumlocution "I lost it." The phrase reveals how men see tears as a betrayal, as treachery by their feelings against their manhood.

As with pain, so with pleasure, sadness, fear, and love. These other feelings may well up from inside and wash over a man, but he must carefully regulate their expression. For the same reason, he may love a woman, but it's unmanly to be passionate.

In *Male Sexuality,* Dr. Bernie Zilbergeld notes that men "learn early that only a narrow range of emotion is permitted . . . aggressiveness, competitiveness, anger, joviality, and the feelings associated with being in control. As we grow older, sexual feelings are added to the list. Weakness, confusion, fear, vulnerability, tenderness, compassion, and sensuality are allowed only to girls and women. A boy who exhibits any such traits is likely to be made fun of and called a sissy or girl (and what could be more devastating?)."

To be a man means never to give in to emotions. A man may be affected by them, but never controlled, never swept along in their currents. Only by controlling his feelings can he master the threats and challenges of life. Reason, not feeling, should be the master.

The closed man is like an actor who never leaves the stage. "Men learn to fake it," says a New York psychiatrist. "They have to fake self-confidence when they are in a panic, knowledge when they are at a loss, interest when they are indifferent, and—more surprising still—orgasm when they're incapable of one." Men must reject, suppress, or ignore their feelings, and search instead for the appropriate response. A man cannot ask himself, "How do I feel?" He must ask, "How am I supposed to feel?"

"My ex-husband hardly ever laughed," says a divorced woman in her late thirties. "He would smile occasionally. I used to tell him, 'Laugh it up, it's cheap and it won't make you fat.' But he was like that. Never got too excited, too sad, too upset. . . . His whole life was strictly meat-and-potatoes, everything bland, blah. Even his emotional involvement in things was like hardtack and water. I kept thinking, 'Here we are at the banquet of life and he's on a diet.' "

Every culture, like every fraternity, has its initiation rites. But there is something different about the "rites of manhood" in this society. Unlike a fraternity initiation, a man's initiation is never over; manhood is never won. Most men exist in a perpetual state of uncertainty about what it means to be a man and whether or not they are living up to that definition.

These are the lessons a young man learns on the playing field, in the movie theater, and on the television screen: to be a man in society means to struggle mightily each day to suppress one's emotions, assert one's independence, cling to one's goals, surpass one's competitors, and the next day, return to begin the struggle again. In some situations, these lessons will stand him in good stead. They will give him strength in an increasingly competitive world; they will give his family a sense of solidity and security.

But even as they make his outer life easier, these lessons of manhood will make his inner life more difficult. For a woman who wants to understand why men can't open up, these lessons are the beginning of an answer.

Debunking the Myths

I **N THE EFFORT** to fathom why men can't open up, a woman will inevitably confront the myths surrounding the closed man. These myths have a variety of sources: history, legend, popular culture, and even science. Men themselves often excuse their inability to communicate by referring to one of these myths. "Every time I make a pitch for him to talk to me," the wife of a young doctor in Minneapolis complained to us, "he says he doesn't have it in him, he's Swedish."

Women too fall back on these myths to explain a man's inability to open up. Frustrated in her efforts to overcome a man's fear of intimacy, a woman may reach for explanations that justify his continuing reticence. Whether they're used by a man as a defense against openness or by a woman as consolation against rejection, the myths surrounding closed men are obstacles on the road to genuine intimacy, obstacles that can be removed with understanding.

The Myth of Male Hormones

Many women—and men—believe that men's fear of emotional intimacy is "just a part of male wiring"; that it's built in, from the start, like factory-installed air conditioning in a car. Just as Lucy, the irascible female in the comic strip *Peanuts,* is crabby because she has "crabby genes," men are closed because they have "closed genes." According to this theory, a man could no more open up than a dog could purr.

"Everyone wants to say that male hormones cause male behavior because they've fallen into an extraordinary trap," says Dr. John Money, director of the Psychohormonal Research Unit at Johns Hopkins in Baltimore. "There really is no such thing as a 'male hormone' in the sense that men have certain hormones that cause them to behave in a certain way.

"There are three hormones [estrogen, testosterone, and progesterone], and both men and women have all three of them. So there are really only 'people' hormones. For example, men don't have a monopoly on feelings of aggression and rage. Have you ever seen a woman—or a lioness or a tigress—try to protect her young? The only thing you can possibly say on this—and it is absolutely scientifically settled—is that there is a threshold that makes it easier for males to defend their territory, to keep it safe from competitors, and rivals, and marauders.

"There is also a difference in threshold that makes it easier for women to be fiercely aggressive in the protection of their young. The difference between the sexes on the issue of emotional reactions, and all others except those related specifically to reproduction and lactation and feeding the young, are differences that are actually sex-shared. The difference lies in the *threshold* for bringing forth that behavior. It doesn't mean either you have it or you don't have it. It's a threshold phenomenon.

"I have some lovely pictures of monkeys," he said. "When a baby monkey was presented to a female, it took only a split second for her to begin parenting it. It was a very dramatic sort of event. You could begin to see immediately a cuddling reaction. You could also see a snarling reaction if someone else approached the young one.

"Then the young one was put in with an older male monkey. He just sat there with sublime indifference while the young one cajoled and pestered him to take notice of it and play with it and be nice to it. The little one kept up his side of the game for a long period of time—about five minutes—until finally the big old male broke down. The message got through to his brain and he finally began doing exactly what the female did."

Although it has only recently been verified by scientific experiments, the nurturing male figure is not new in popular culture. The Academy-award-winning film *Kramer vs. Kramer* is about a distant, indifferent father, preoccupied with his career until the departure of his wife and the stubborn prodding of his son elicit from him the loving, nurturing response typical of mothers. Like the old male monkey, the father's threshold for nurturing behavior is higher.

The same theme runs throughout popular fiction, movies, children's stories, and folklore: the grumpy, lonely man, first pestered, then won by a child's persistent need for love. From Dickens's *A Christmas Carol* to *Little Orphan Annie*, the myth of male hormones, the myth that men are *naturally* cold and unreachable, has been rejected again and again. Men may require an extra push or a longer pull, but they can and do cross the threshold into emotional intimacy.

In the same way, a man can respond to a woman's need for intimacy. According to Dr. Money, it may require more external stimuli, or more sustained stimuli, to elicit the response in him than in her, because her threshold for intimacy behavior is lower than his. But if she pursues the same response in him, eventually he will respond. The potential *is* there.

The Myth of the Breadwinner

"I think my sons have an easier time than I did," a former Navy officer in San Diego told us. "I think this liberation business is better for everyone. You can act more like yourself. But to tell you the truth, I think there's a point beyond which it just can't go. When you come right down to it, men and women are just built different."

This is the cornerstone of the breadwinner myth: men and women are just built different. As the stronger sex, men are designed to protect and provide for their families. Women, the weaker sex, are designed for maintaining the home and nurturing the young. Because of these different, "natural" roles, the argument goes, men and women have developed different personalities. Men are hard because the world in which they must compete is hard. Women are soft because they are—and always have been—protected from the hardness of the outside world. The need to be hard prevents men from showing vulnerability. The need to perform the nurturing tasks allows women to be open.

Recent research, however, indicates that the distinction between Man the Breadwinner and Woman the Homemaker is relatively new, that men are not naturally hard and aggressive any more than women are naturally soft and nurturing. In *Masculinity and Femininity,* two psychologists at the University of Texas, Janet T. Spence and Robert L. Helmreich, traced the development of sex roles through history. They found that in agricultural societies (the U.S. was an agricultural society until early in this century) there was too much work to be done, in the field and in the kitchen, to excuse women simply on the basis of muscular weakness. Women not only baked the bread, they helped harvest the wheat.

As the industrial revolution swept poor farm families out of the countryside and into the city, few could afford to let an able-bodied woman tend the family without generating additional income at home or in the marketplace. Both husband and wife were forced to take jobs.

As industrialization spread and more poor families worked their way into the middle class, "the economic contribution of increasing proportions of women was to be found solely within the home. The division along sexual lines between instrumental and expressive functions was thrown into high relief and, along with it, expectations that women and men possess contrasting personal qualities."

Spence and Helmreich's conclusion is that sex roles are not immutable; that they are not tied to muscles, sex organs, or any other fact of human anatomy; that they change, sometimes radically and rapidly, with time and circumstances. It's only within the last several generations that women have come to play the "nurturing, stay-at-home" role and men the "go-out-and-face-the-world" role that some people now see as "natural."

Because men and women now play more similar roles in the work force, there is no longer any basis for the different roles they play elsewhere—at home or in relationships. The roles of the breadwinner and the homemaker as they developed over the last fifty years, and the notion that certain activities, certain roles, and certain personalities are traditionally masculine or feminine, have passed into myth.

Just as women can be aggressive as well as nurturing, ambitious as well as motherly, men can be nurturing as well as competitive, open as well as closed. A man's body doesn't condemn him to the role of breadwinner and the hard, unexpressive life that it implies. In human behavior, adaptability is the only constant.

The Myth of the Latin Lover

According to this myth, men with "Latin" ethnic and geographic affiliations are more open and more capable of intimacy than men from other regions. Whether they're Greek, Italian, Spanish, or from some other "southern" region, they are almost automatically more emotional and more expressive.

The other side of this myth is that men of British and Scandinavian backgrounds, like the countries they come from, are colder or more closed than other men. Women in relationships with emotionally reticent men sometimes blame their reticence on their ethnicity. "My husband is a cold, New England WASP, through and through," a Boston housewife told us with a sigh of resignation. "When his parents come over, I swear the temperature in this house drops ten degrees."

The myth of the Latin lover is invoked to explain a wide variety of emotional differences, from temper to temperament, from hand gestures to emotional openness. The experts, however, doubt these explanations. "Latin men don't necessarily fear emotional intimacy any less than 'northerners,'" says psychiatrist Virginia Sadock. "There may be more demonstrativeness, but the expression of vulnerability is just as guarded."

Dr. Alan Stone of Harvard suggests that "Latin" men actually have more difficulty expressing vulnerability than other men because of an exaggerated macho self-image. "In many cultures in which men seem to be the most open," said Stone, "the image of machismo interferes with openness on other fronts."

Ultimately, ethnicity does nothing more than mark the boundaries of a man's emotional life; it helps shape the *style* of his relationships. A Greek, an Italian, or a Spaniard might be much better than an Englishman, a Scandinavian, or an American WASP at expressing his love for a woman. He may make extravagant protestations of love where a northerner would only smile shyly and stare at the floor. But making a meaningful connection is not easy for either.

The lesson of the myth of the Latin lover is that understanding emotional styles can help a woman adjust to the emotional needs and capabilities of a man. For example, a man from a traditional WASP background may never feel comfortable with the grand romantic gestures of the stereotypical Latin lover, but that doesn't mean he's incapable of the grand passion behind the gesture. "Love is like a bridge game," one woman told us. "Everybody has their own style of play. You have to adjust a little to your partner's style, and he has to adjust a little to yours, if you want to make a grand slam."

The Myth of the Blue-Collar Chauvinist

According to this myth, the blue-collar male is forced to compensate for his lack of material success by affirming his masculinity in other ways. Because he can't be controlling and independent in his work life, he plays the closed man even more intensely in his emotional life.

In an episode of television's "All in the Family," Archie and Edith Bunker are invited to the wedding of Edith's cousin. Edith is eager to go, but Archie refuses. In a rare fit of independence that startles Archie, Edith attends the wedding without him, leaving him alone in the house for a weekend. Within hours, Archie is despondent. Although he would never admit it, he can't live without Edith. On the telephone with her, he tries desperately to conceal his loneliness and frustration. But he isn't above trying to make her feel guilty. He plays the suffering husband to her frivolous, irresponsible wife: there's no one to care for the house, no one to cook his meals. The ploy works. Edith cuts short her visit and returns to Archie's reproving embrace. He cautions her about shirking her wifely duties again, then wriggles out of her arms and demands his dinner.

For most of the seventies, "All in the Family" *was* blue-collar America. The blue-collar woman was Edith Bunker: flighty, motherly, slightly dim-witted, but heroically loving. The blue-collar man was Archie: suspicious, complaining, selfish, and unloving except in unspoken ways. Their marriage, lopsided as it was, became the stereotype of blue-collar relationships.

According to the myth, the blue-collar male demands obedience from his wife and children. In typical Archie Bunker fashion, he stands on his prerogatives in the house (the best chair), insists on routine (dinner on time), and treats even the slightest deviation as domestic treason. He expects, in the words of writer Andrew Tolson, "the old 'pipe and slippers' routine."

"Working-class masculinity becomes a kind of 'performance,'" says Tolson. The man "develops a repertoire of stories, jokes, and routines. He expresses himself, not so much in an inner, compulsive struggle for achievement, as through a collective toughness, a masculine 'performance.' " Other emotions—love, kindness, gentleness—are not part of the act.

Many experts, however, now believe that the blue-collar man's reputation is undeserved. Recent studies have shown that, while white-collar men are more likely to advocate "liberated" sex roles, blue-collar men are more receptive to change. In a study of sex roles conducted by Dr. John De Frain of the University of Nebraska, blue-collar men— "electricians, plumbers, bull-dozer operators"—did 20 percent of the housework, while white-collar men did only 5 percent.

"The blue-collar guy often has less power in his job," concludes Dr. De Frain, "so he tends to put on a real macho face in public. He will swagger around and boast about wearing the pants in his family. But when he gets home, he tends to let the barriers down."

There is comfort in myths: they justify the perpetuation of behavior we think we can't change. Some men find comfort in the myth that they're denied intimacy simply because they were born male. Some women prefer to believe the myth that they're excluded from intimacy with men because of men's genes, history, ethnicity, or social class, rather than face the possibility that they've been accomplices in their own exclusion.

However comforting the myths surrounding a closed man may be, debunking them is the first step in better understanding the *real* reasons for his emotional reticence.

The Ulysses
Syndrome

Men's Fear of Dependence

*I*N GREEK MYTHOLOGY, Ulysses was the king of
Ithaca and the shrewdest of the Greek leaders in
the Trojan War. It was Ulysses who devised the
plan to end the ten-year siege of Troy by building
the Trojan horse, secretly filling it with soldiers,
and offering it to the Trojans as an acknowledgment of defeat. The Trojans brought the horse into the city, and the
Greeks poured out to surprise and defeat them. Ulysses was
acclaimed a hero.

But the story of Ulysses as told by Homer in the *Odys-
sey* begins after the fall of Troy. Blown off course by the
storm-wrath of an angry god, Ulysses wanders the Mediterranean Sea for twenty years in search of home. Of the many
trials that he and his crew endure, the most dangerous is the
passage through the Straits of Messina. The jagged shores
on both sides of the straits are inhabited by sirens who sing
so beautifully, so seductively, that no man can hear their
song and not be drawn toward it. Hundreds of ships and
thousands of sailors have perished in this narrow passage,
lured onto the sharp rocks by the sirens' irresistible song.

To save his ship from the crowded graveyard at the
sirens' feet, Ulysses instructs his men to fill their ears with

beeswax to deafen them against the sirens' beckoning. He orders the crew to lash him to the mast and tie a gag over his mouth. He would hear the sirens, but he would not respond. As the sirens sing and Ulysses writhes in agony and frustration, the ship passes safely through the straits.

A Latter-Day Ulysses. The closed man is a latter-day Ulysses. Like the Greek king, he is attracted by the seductive promises of women, calling from the shores of emotional intimacy for him to join them. Yet he fears the consequences if he succumbs to their entreaties. He's afraid that the ship of his masculinity—the vessel that carries him through the hardships and storms of a man's life—will be torn apart if he allows himself to be drawn off course by the sweet song of intimacy with a woman. So, despite his urge to follow, despite his urge to call out in response, he ties himself to the mast of his masculinity, puts a gag firmly in his mouth, and sails by.

Do men really like women? That is the unspoken question that comes through loud and clear whenever women complain—to survey takers, to psychiatrists, to marriage counselors, or to divorce lawyers—about closed men. They may love women; they may want sexual intimacy with women; but do they really want the kind of easy familiarity and acceptance that would make genuine emotional sharing so much easier?

When a man won't communicate his feelings in a relationship, it's hardly surprising that a woman begins to wonder just how much affection is buried beneath that silence. "I don't question that he loves me," says a woman in Kansas City who's been married for twelve years, "I just wonder sometimes if he *likes* me. If he had a choice of whom to spend his time with, would it be me? When you get married for love, as we did, that's no guarantee that twelve years down the road you're going to really like each other."

"After years of treating men," says Dr. Theodore Isaac Rubin, "I've come to realize that a great many men really do not like women. They've been taught in innumerable and often subtle ways to consider [women] predatory and manipulative while at the same time seeing them as subservient, lacking strength of character, and generally falling into the category of intellectual lightweights. This negative paradox, coupled to undesired feminine feelings and dependence on women, must lead to hostility."

What we discovered in the course of researching this book was that emotional aloofness in men is often based less on the dislike women may imagine than on the fear that it usually masks. Many men fear intimacy with women, both because of the sexual challenge it represents and the invitation to dependence that it offers. We call this fear of intimacy —and the pattern of problems that usually occurs in a relationship because of it—the Ulysses Syndrome.

Dr. Ari Kiev, a psychiatrist and director of the Social Psychiatry Research Institute in Manhattan, described to us a female patient of his—we'll call her Barbara—who was contemplating leaving her lover, Joe, with whom she had been living for several years. Barbara learned that he had been married for seven years, had divorced, and lived alone for a year. He still seemed to her "very needful." But as soon as they began to live together, their relationship began to slip into an uncomfortable pattern.

Because she saw him as needful, Barbara started taking care of Joe. She did all the things his wife had refused to do: she ran errands for him, planned events she thought he would enjoy, gave him breakfast in bed on weekends, arranged her social life to make the most time for him. Instead of feeling grateful and closer, however, Joe perceived in those acts of generosity an implied request for deeper intimacy and soon began to feel resentful and distant. Barbara weathered the climate of hostility and the occasional storms of anger, but she couldn't understand why, after all her efforts, Joe should withdraw from her and display an animosity she had never seen before they started living together.

As a result, Barbara became increasingly depressed and started leaning on Joe for emotional support and reassurance. Joe, of course, perceived that "leaning" as a renewed demand for closeness, thereby triggering another round of withdrawal and resentment. It was to get off this "not-so-merry-go-round" that Barbara went to Dr. Kiev.

According to him, Barbara's increased demands threw her lover into a state of confusion and fear. "He felt neglected by his previous wife, and rejected by her, but he still couldn't deal with Barbara's constant demands for intimacy," Kiev told us.

Like most closed men, Joe was torn between the demands of manhood and his need for intimacy. On the one hand, as a man, he had to strive for independence, both financial and emotional. Thus, there was always a part of him that wanted to break away from the relationship. On the other hand, he secretly longed for the security of emotional dependence, which life with Barbara offered.

He couldn't surrender openly to that longing, however, because he feared the loss of masculinity and the possibility of rejection that, in his mind, were associated with dependence. After all, letting himself become dependent on his wife had only led to hurt. Instead of blaming his wife or himself for their failed relationship, he retreated further into manly isolation. To fulfill his secret need for intimacy, to sail toward the siren call, was to risk rejection and ultimately to betray his manhood.

Caught in this dilemma, simultaneously drawn toward intimacy and toward the ideals and safety of masculinity, Joe accepted dependence by staying with Barbara but masked that surrender with feelings of resentment, feelings which protected him from rejection and allowed him to preserve his sense of manhood. Secretly longing for Barbara's emotional support, he blamed her for bringing out that "demasculinizing" need in him.

Barbara and Joe's problems are typical of the problems created by men's fear of dependence. They are not problems of feeling or intention. Barbara and Joe felt deeply for each other, and both had every intention of making a permanent and fulfilling relationship. Their problems did not emerge at first; relationships that suffer from the Ulysses Syndrome often start out healthy and promising.

Barbara and Joe's problems began when Joe's fear of dependence caused him to resist both Barbara's need and his own need for intimacy. That self-punishing resistance produced feelings of hostility and resentment that pushed their relationship into a downward spiral. For them, as for many couples caught in this kind of spiral, the first step in breaking it is to understand the fear that set it in motion.

Behind the Fear

Although few men are man enough to admit it, many of them envy the emotional fluency women bring to relationships. "More than one man," says New York psychiatrist Dr. David Peretz, "has told me that if he were ever reincarnated, he'd like to come back as a woman. He was tired of fighting the world and longed to have someone else take care of him emotionally." The man was tired, in other words, of masculine independence and envied the opportunity to admit dependence and accept intimacy, an opportunity that he thought was available only to women.

If men long for emotional intimacy, why are they afraid to give in to it? Drawing heavily on Freud, many experts argue that a boy's primary deprivation and deepest hurt is the emotional separation from his mother. His efforts to cope with this separation, to break off his identification with her, to reconcile his love for her with his feelings of rejection and estrangement—these efforts often affect the rest of his emotional life.

According to Freudian psychoanalytic theory, the separation from the mother resolves one important aspect of the Oedipal conflict. A boy must surrender his sexual impulses toward his mother, under threat of castration by his father; make an identification with his father, the power figure; and eventually return to his mother in a nonsexual relationship. This entire process, of course, takes place not in "real life" but in the unconscious fantasy life of the child.

When this process of separation goes awry, a boy's ability to form intimate relationships in later life is often adversely affected. If, for example, a boy fails to separate adequately from his mother, he may remain sexually, seductively involved with her. "Intimacy in adult life is then equated with the childhood wish for intimacy with the Oedipal object," says sex therapist Helen Singer Kaplan, M.D., "and is therefore avoided." If, on the other hand, a boy fails to make a sufficient identification with his father, he may ultimately reject intimacy with women for fear of becoming effeminate.

The Freudian Oedipal analysis is helpful in understanding the roots of men's fear of dependence, but it's not essential. "You don't have to accept Freudian theory," says Dr. Peretz, "to recognize that every man has been deeply hurt by a woman at some time in his life, and that woman is his mother. No woman can provide a child with everything that child wants at all times. After all, every woman has other demands on her attention: a husband, a job, perhaps, or other children. And at times, her own wishes and fears conflict with the needs and wishes of the child." Whenever a mother fails to satisfy these desires, inevitably there is hurt and disappointment.

"People develop fears of intimacy in adult life," says Kaplan, "because of negative and disappointing experiences with intimate relationships in early childhood. They never develop what Erikson has called 'basic trust' toward their parents, their first intimates, during their critical childhood period."

Some men are more fortunate than others: they negotiate the separation from their mothers successfully and still keep part of their mothers within them. But the closed man isn't so successful. When he makes the emotional break with his mother, he feels contradictory impulses. Part of him longs for the acceptance and dependence of the lost mother-son relationship; part of him rejects those feelings and strives to develop a "masculine" personality, which becomes largely a negative activity, a matter of rejecting the feminine within himself. He may even generalize these negative feelings to a hatred and fear of all women.

Because of this split between his desire for intimacy and his fear of it, a closed man's emotional behavior is often characterized by fiercely contrary emotions; he both longs for intimacy and rejects it. When faced with an emotional challenge, he may be thrown into what psychologists call an "approach-avoidance" conflict: a part of him wants to come closer and establish intimacy; part will reject any offer of intimacy as undermining his masculinity.

To protect himself from the frustration and anxiety generated by such double-bind conflicts, a man develops self-protective mechanisms of emotional detachment. He learns not to care, not to put himself in a position that might create painful inner conflict. He also learns to fear intimacy with anyone who might force him into such conflicts.

The fear of intimacy and the dependence that it represents seldom show themselves as fear. Concealing fear is part of the masculine personality that the closed man is trying to effect. Thus, the Ulysses Syndrome is characterized by the sublimation of fear into forms that are appropriately masculine: devaluation, hostility, and indifference.

Devaluation. The devaluation of women and female attributes is one way in which a traditionally male-dominated society has learned to cope with the fear of intimacy. That devaluation usually begins in the family. Dr. Ruth E. Hartley, who studied the relative status of men and women in the home, writes about how many children see their parents: "[M]en mostly do what they want to do and are very important. In the family, they are the boss; they have authority in relation to the disposal of monies and they get first choice in the use of the most comfortable chair in the house and the daily paper. They seem to get mad a lot, but are able to make children feel good; they laugh and make jokes more than women do. Compared with mothers, fathers are more fun to be with; they are exciting to have around; they have the best ideas."

Women, on the other hand, are often seen as "fearful" and "indecisive"; also "physically weak, squeamish about seeing blood, unadventurous, more easily hurt and killed than men, and afraid of getting wet or getting an electric shock." They "have a way of doing things the wrong way." In emergencies, they scream instead of taking charge; they fuss over their children's grades.

Just as mothers are often seen as second-class adults, girls are seen as second-class kids. Boys are quick to recognize that girls usually live under different rules. They perceive girls' activities as more restricted; their play more timid; their sports more gentle. While boys can wander more or less at will, their games ranging over whole neighborhoods from dawn until after dusk, girls stay close to home, reestablish parental contact often, and have curfews. Girls are also traditionally precluded from rough games and general roving.

Despite advances in the status of women since Dr. Hartley's studies, the stigma in many children's eyes remains. For example, recent studies have shown that in nursery school it is common for little girls to wish they were boys. They have simply come to the realization, says Dr. Robert E. Gould, that "boys have it so much better in the world." Those early intimations of inferiority often last into adulthood. Surveys show that most women want their first child to be a son; and, if limited to one child, they want it to be a boy.

By devaluing women in general, a man can justify his own inability (disguised as unwillingness) to make himself vulnerable to a specific woman in a relationship that must be both equal and reciprocal to be truly intimate. A man may also devalue his own wife or lover specifically. "If a single person has an intimacy problem, he will get to a certain point of closeness with a new partner and then lose interest," says Helen Singer Kaplan. "When he first meets her, she is wonderful. But when the relationship reaches that magic point, he begins to focus on her shortcomings and grows disenchanted. These people have an endless series of relationships which always end at roughly the same point."

Hostility. Sometimes men react to intimacy with feelings of hostility. The fear that women will "trap" men in intimacy is deeply ingrained in our culture and shows itself in many forms: from Eve's betrayal of Adam to Scarlett O'Hara's betrayal of Rhett Butler. The Greek goddess of love, Aphrodite, betrayed her husband, Hephaestus, who was lame (symbolically impotent), by having an affair with a macho, "closed" god, Aries, the god of war.

This distrust has become a fixture of popular culture. "Little girls want pretty things and pretty smells and to be cuddled and kissed," warns the frivolous, best-selling sex guide for men, *The Sensuous Man,* with thinly veiled hostility, "but most of all they want to be wives. *Your* wants are more basic, so you may weaken and let a promise slip off your tongue while you're panting heavily with desire. And then you're dead. And you deserve it."

When men speak of women who are searching for husbands, they often revert to the hostile language of the hunted talking about the hunter: "She bagged him." "She set a trap for him." "She finally caught one." "She landed him." "She got her man." "He's quite a catch/prize/find." In a postwedding receiving line, it is generally considered improper to say "congratulations" to the bride. The forbidden implication is that, after stalking a husband at length, she has finally nabbed one—lucky woman.

The more directly a man is confronted with emotions by a woman, the more he may feel ambushed. "[Women] use tears as weapon," warns *The Sensuous Man* with characteristic hostility. "They'll use tears to badger you, pressure you, make you feel like a heel, or distract from their own feelings. They'll cry when they want something. They'll cry when they don't want something. They'll cry every time you do *anything* not precisely in keeping with their desires."

By assuming an adversarial role in relationships with

women, men avoid the compromises and accommodations that would be required if women were treated as allies in the common pursuit of intimacy. In this view, intimacy can be had *either* on his terms or on her terms. The former is seen as a victory, the latter as a defeat.

Indifference. Occasionally a man's fear of dependence is masked by an offhand, seemingly careless attitude toward relationships with women. Some men like to think of themselves as above the "petty pleasures and hurts" of intimacy. In this indifference, they may find protection from its hurts, but they also cut themselves off from its pleasures.

"It's not that men don't like women," says Cathy, thirty-one, a fund-raising consultant in New York who spends most of her working day with men. "They just don't have much in common with them. When men aren't being sensitive to women's feelings, when they don't pick up on women's needs in sex, it's a matter of indifference. They don't care. Women don't matter. You should see how much men in business situations try to appeal to other businessmen. If they made half that effort with women, they'd have no trouble."

Whether it takes the form of locker-room ridicule or boardroom indifference, hostility or devaluation, the fear of dependence is one of the most important forces preventing the closed man from sharing intimacy with a woman. It is the rope that binds him, like Ulysses, to the mast of his masculinity. It is a psychological bind that begins in childhood and, if allowed to develop, becomes increasingly hard to break.

The hold that the fear of dependence has on a man *can* be broken, however. Understanding the role of his mother in his early emotional development is important, but there are other players whose roles must also be understood before a man can begin to break the psychological grip of the past and overcome the fears that keep him from enjoying genuine intimacy.

His Father, Himself

I **F A MAN** can't express his emotions or share intimacy, his relationship with his mother is probably part of the reason—but only part. Experts are just beginning to see that a man's father, as much as or more than his mother, plays a crucial role in his ability to open up.

Mothers have always known that sons watch their fathers keenly. During the 1970s, a series of studies began to explore just how fathers influence their sons. Work by Judith and Leonard Worrell established that a man is more likely to dominate his wife in a stereotypically chauvinistic way if his father dominated him in a stereotypically partriarchal way. Men who cling to traditional attitudes toward wife and home had fathers who clung to the same values, who exercised absolute power within the family.

"Certainly, it's a very good start if the man has had a genuinely loving mother," psychiatrist Virginia Sadock told us, "but it is equally and perhaps even more essential that his father be someone with whom he can identify—so that he enjoys being a man, so that he thinks being a man is a good thing to be, so that he has his father's approval."

For too many sons, fathers are drill instructors in the

boot camp of "learning to be a man." The lessons of manhood are the ones fathers teach. Boys see themselves in their fathers: the men they will be, the men they want to be. For a boy, manhood begins and ends with his father. By inspiration, by punishment, by example, by accident—a father teaches his son what it means to be a man.

"If you have a father who never hugged you," says Dr. Sadock, "who never played baseball with you, who never did anything with you, what you think is, 'He doesn't like me.' But if you have a father who never expressed his feelings, you think, 'My god, men never do that.' And it makes you think there's something wrong with you if you do yourself."

Although most fathers try to be good parents, many of them fall into one (or both) of two patterns of behavior: the *demanding father,* who by his relentless expectations and disapproval leads his son to believe that "he doesn't like me"; and the cold, distant, *ungiving father,* who teaches his son, by example, that a man *should* be cold. Whichever father a man has, his ability to share his feelings, to achieve intimacy and to give love—to men or women—is ultimately his father's handiwork no less than his mother's.

"He Doesn't Like Me": The Demanding Father. "I was always a little afraid of my father," a young man in Dayton, Ohio, told us, "at least until he had his first stroke. Now, finally, he's my friend. I think most men hope their children will outdo them. But they have no way of expressing that, so they show disapproval."

No one in a man's life will ever expect more of him than his father. Whether those expectations have been stated in words, shouted to the world, or just kept in the privacy of a father's heart, they are part of the paternal bond, and have been since the father sat in the hospital waiting room and heard, "It's a boy." Just as a boy thinks his father is capable of doing everything except wrong, a father is sure that his son will do everything right. Expectations are the hard currency of love between many fathers and sons.

Unfortunately, the same expectations that fill a relationship with joy and warmth one day can fill it with disappointment and chill the next. "My father never mentioned my achievements in college," said a twenty-seven-year-old man in Boston who conducts regional musical theater, "but he was enthusiastic about my plans for business school. Then, when I went to music school instead, he never commented about how well I did. He only cared about what kind of job I would get and how much I'd get paid. Now I'm working and getting a good salary, and he doesn't want to talk about that. He wants to know where I plan to go from here. It's a never-ending cycle. I'll never catch up with where he wants me to be."

Some men respond to this cycle of expectation and disappointment by withdrawing. If a son resents his father's demands fiercely, he may strike back with his most potent weapon, failure. Disappointed by his son's failure to satisfy his expectations, a father, too, may become distant and resentful. A cold war of indifference may set in.

Other men respond to a father's demands with fear. They continue to struggle against his expectations, but the renewing sense of failure undermines both their love for their fathers and their own self-respect. This was brought home to us in a business conversation with a thirty-year-old New York lawyer who shares a practice with his father. "I'd better take notes," the lawyer told us in the heat of negotiations. "If I don't, my father will break my fingers."

These feelings of withdrawal and fear can sometimes impair a man's ability to participate in a satisfying emotional relationship. He may become suspicious of intimacy in general, or he may associate masculine behavior with emotional distance. A man who has a good relationship with his father, on the other hand, and consequently a strong masculine identity, may have less fear that intimacy will somehow lure him into effeminacy.

"Men Never Do That": The Ungiving Father. A father's expectations are often childlike in their unreality: they're a fantasy of self-fulfillment. It's almost inevitable that a son faced with these fantastic expectations will fail in his father's eyes. Most men are not trained to cope with *any* failure, but the failure of a son is a father's very special pain.

A man who works as an administrative assistant to a South Side Boston politician reminisced about his father: "Every night after work, he'd just sit around and watch TV, never saying a word. But he somehow managed to communicate to me, in a very powerful way, that I could please him only if I did better than he did in life."

Some fathers rebuke their sons for failure with blows. Others use words. Still others use the most insidious and devastating of all possible punishments, the withdrawal of love. Unlike a mother's love, which is usually all-consuming and all-forgiving—a love that doesn't depend on achievement—a father's love is often demanding, unforgiving, and conditional; an emotion akin to respect. Like respect, a father's love must be earned. When it's not earned, when a son fails to live up to his father's demands, it's withdrawn.

The withdrawal of love is a common feature of father-son relationships. It's why many men see their fathers as closed, uncommunicative, and unloving. Janet Wolfe, Ph.D., associate director of the Institute for Rational Emotive Therapy, told us: "People fill out a biographical form when they come here, and nine out of ten of them describe their mothers as warm and kind and their fathers as cold and distant. They say their fathers didn't talk very much and didn't relate very much."

According to Herb Goldberg, author of *The Hazards of Being Male,* fathers are "typically absent, uninvolved, or emotionally passive when present." While still keen-eyed boys, men see this pattern of behavior in their fathers. Because the father is often the only adult male in a boy's life, his behavior usually becomes a model of the way men *should* act.

The ultimate withdrawal of love, of course, is absence. Some sons seldom see their fathers. Emotional distance is underscored by physical distance. For a child who learned at his mother's breast that physical closeness and love are inseparable, a father's absence is the final proof of his disapproval. The distance and disapproval combine to begin the cycle again: love, loss, longing, love.

By withdrawing love, by being emotionally cold and ungiving, a father conveys two of the most important lessons of manhood. The lesson of coldness is independence. Just as battling the elements will make a boy strong and resourceful, some fathers believe, living in the cold fresh air of indifference will make him emotionally self-reliant. He'll learn to live in a world of uncaring and uncared-for people. He'll be able to persevere alone—the natural state for a man. If he's dependent, either physically or emotionally, he can't cut his own path or make his own decisions. Emotional hardship is as good for a man as physical hardship. Present adversity prepares him for future adversity.

The second lesson of an ungiving father is self-protection. Just as the father protects himself from disappointment in his son's failures by withdrawing, the son must learn to cut emotional losses by reducing the chances they will occur. If nothing is extended, nothing can be cut off. "A man," said Ernest Hemingway, "should never put himself in a position to lose what he cannot afford to lose." If a man doesn't care about another person, he can't be hurt by the fallibility or withdrawal of that person.

By not extending love to his son, a father teaches him that "men never do that"—that men don't offer love to others; they wait for it to be offered to them. A son's repeated efforts to fulfill his father's impossible expectations are, ultimately, offerings of love. By rejecting them, a father tells his son: "It's appropriate for men to reject offerings of love—just as I have rejected yours." For this reason, some men can't love anyone until they feel they've won their father's love.

Steve: *My Father, My Friend.* Perhaps because I enjoyed such an unusually close relationship with my father, the intellectual discovery that fathers play an important role in their sons' emotional development came as no surprise to me. As a child growing up in out-of-the-way places, moving every few years to some new, temporary home, I inevitably turned to my father—one of the few constants in my life—more than most boys do.

But our closeness was also my father's doing. He and his own father had had a distant relationship. The youngest son in a family of six children, separated by forty years and the competing demands of a rural life, my father hardly knew his father. Unlike some men, who pass on their father's gift —whether it's love or indifference—like a baton to their sons, my father gave me the intimacy that he had never been able to have with his father.

He was as much friend as father. I remember a child-hood filled with activities: building a dollhouse for my sister, buying jewelry at the *souk* for my mother, hiking and camping in our Lone Scout Troop with its roster of two.

After I began spending most of the year at school in the States, vacations became special. When I flew in for Christmas or the summer, my father would always take off from work so we could spend precious time together. My fondest memory is of my father knocking at my door, when I overslept after a long plane flight, and saying impatiently, "I want you to come out and play."

Perhaps because my father and I have always been so close, I have studied relationships between men and their fathers with special interest. While ours is hardly the only example of mutual respect and support, I have been surprised at how many relationships between fathers and sons are marked by fear, disrespect, and indifference; and how few sons feel with their fathers the bond I feel with mine.

"Talk to Me." Among closed men, the typical father-son relationship is closer to that described in John Steinbeck's novel *East of Eden*. Cal, the rebellious son, longs to be loved by his stern, authoritarian father. He even tries to buy his father's love, by raising beans and lending his father the

profits. He searches vainly for some other relationship to satisfy his need to be loved, but only his father's approval will give him the emotional fulfillment he craves. At one point, in desperation, he pleads for some sign of love from his father. "Talk to me!" he cries. "Talk to me."

Many men pass through childhood certain of a mother's love but uncertain of a father's. For that very reason, a father's love takes on exaggerated importance. It becomes, in a boy's eyes, the ultimate test of worthiness and acceptance.

It also becomes the model of love for a man's other relationships. He will continue to mimic his father's coldness and indifference in response to love, whether it's offered by a man or a woman. Just as his father stood quiet and ungiving when his son cried out, the son will stand immovable when someone who loves him cries out, "Talk to me. Talk to me."

Boys' Night Out

Is He Closer to Other Men?

> The perfect friendship of two men is the deepest and highest sentiment of which the finite mind is capable; women miss the best in life.
>
> GERTRUDE FRANKLIN ATHERTON,
> *The Conqueror* (1902)

ACTRESS JOANNE WOODWARD, who is also the wife of Paul Newman, was once asked about the extraordinarily close relationship her husband developed with Robert Redford during the filming of *Butch Cassidy and the Sundance Kid,* and later *The Sting.* Woodward replied: "When those two get together, forget opening your mouth if you happen to be female. Bob and Paul really do have a chemistry. Someday, Paul and Bob will run off together. And I'll be left behind with Lola Redford."

A strong friendship between two men possesses, both in history and in common perception, the power of magic. History, mythology, and literature sparkle with examples of extraordinary camaraderie, self-sacrifice in the face of danger, and undying devotion between two men. From Huck Finn and Tom Sawyer, Tonto and the Lone Ranger, Butch Cassidy and the Sundance Kid, Captain Kirk and Mr. Spock to the Dukes of Hazard, legend continues to portray close friendships between two men as more selfless, more intimate, and more enduring than relationships between men and women could ever be.

According to legend, when the world is unforgiving, when women are too demanding, when the struggle is too much to carry on alone, a man seeks the companionship of another man. Whether they travel to the Wild West, to a cabin in the mountains, or just to a local bar or bowling alley, close male friends together create their own special world. Where there are women, there is responsibility; where there are men, there is freedom.

Many women share Joanne Woodward's nagging suspicion that men share with each other things they will not share with the opposite sex. A woman can feel inadequate when she compares her husband's commitment to his Monday Night Football gang or Thursday-night poker game to his commitment to her. But the reality of male friendships, especially within groups, doesn't always live up to the legend.

Phyllis, the wife of an insurance salesman in Dallas named Ed, told us about her encounter with real-life friendships between men. She became slightly insecure when, after three years of "relatively happy" marriage, Ed began to spend one night out a week with Jim, an old friend from college. "Is Ed closer to Jim than he is to me?" she wondered. Gradually, the evenings with Jim became more frequent and lasted later into the night.

Phyllis knew that Ed was having problems at the office: his job was up for review, and his supervisor had given him a bad rating. But he had resisted talking about it with her. "I began to worry that it was easier for Ed to talk to Jim than to me," Phyllis told us. "It actually made me jealous. Finally, we discussed it, and it turned out I was wrong." Ed went out drinking with Jim to *forget* his problems, Phyllis discovered, not to share them. He hardly mentioned them to Jim. "I wasn't jealous anymore," says Phyllis, "but I was mad at Jim for not being any help.

"Just look at most men. They're supposed to be great buddies, and die together in wars and everything. But how many of them have any *real* friends? They have guys they can play golf with, and even borrow money from, but they don't have friends they can call up for support—emotional support—when they need it."

In a letter to Dear Abby in 1983, a woman in Minneapolis complained that when her husband was hospitalized for a serious illness, none of his "friends" from the office ever came to visit him; only *her* friends visited. Abby's response was simple: men don't make real friends.

The most skeptical view of male friendships comes from anthropologist Margaret Mead. Hearing stories about emotional intimacy and openness between soldiers on the front line in the Second World War Mead decided to study these man-to-man relationships more carefully and see how intimate they really were.

She concluded that the closeness of men under fire was not based on mutual interests or shared emotions, but on solidarity in the face of danger. It was an arbitrary, undiscriminating closeness. According to Mead, pairs of men who described themselves as "best friends" were inevitably bunkmates, tank mates, or foxhole mates. They were drawn together by the common experience of loneliness and danger. These special male relationships, Mead felt, were "accidents of association," not based on "special personality characteristics," and therefore were not "capable of ripening into real friendship." She compared their intimacy to that of car-wreck or flood victims, not of two people caring for each other in an alliance of love.

The reality of male friendships lies somewhere between the embarrassing enthusiasm of Gertrude Franklin Atherton and the scientific skepticism of Margaret Mead. Both of these women, like so many women, miss the essence of what men find in their inarticulate, informal, and sometimes outright lazy friendships with other men.

"I feel comfortable with other men," says a thirty-two-year-old man in Los Angeles who gets together with a group of other men every Thursday night for softball games, "but not too comfortable. There's always a little edge of competition, and that makes it sharp and exhilarating." The pattern of male friendship is usually established early in a man's life. For many men, relationships with women during these early years are a roller-coaster ride. Being with "one of the guys" allows a man to release built-up tensions and reinforce his sense of sexual identity.

For the rest of his life, a man will use his friendships with other men as a way of escaping from the demands of the world, a way of re-creating the comfortable, unpressured world that he associates (not always accurately) with adolescence, the idyllic time before job and family and responsibility. "You've seen those beer commercials," says a New York psychiatrist. "That's not the way men are together or ever were. But it's the way they *think* they were, and that's all that matters. Two men may be sitting at a bar and saying one word every ten minutes, but in their minds they're in one of those beer commercials."

A man in his fifties in Chicago told us about his best friend from high-school days, a man who now lives in New York. They talk on the phone every few weeks, and rendezvous back in their home town as often as possible—even if their wives can't make it. "Being with Joe is like being in a time warp," he said. "I see my whole life in front of me at one time. He knows me right straight through, from first page to last, by heart. Of course, we follow each other's work, we don't just sit around and reminisce. We argue politics and go to the ball game. We do what we've always done, and that's the point."

Another man described for us the deep loss he felt when his best friend died. "I'll be eighty-one in May, but my birthday won't be the same without Dan. Every year, the first three weeks in May, we'd take off and go up to the French River in Canada. Dan had a cabin way back upriver. We'd get there just before the ice broke up, just in time to see the birds come back, the grass turn green. It was the best time of year. Both our birthdays were in May and we'd celebrate them there. Dan made these cakes. Awful little things—he always used too much booze. But I ate them. We'd take the boat out and sit and fish. We talked mostly. We always had the whole year to catch up on.

"Dan died last year, just a few weeks after we came back from the river. We'd been going up there for sixty years, every year, three weeks—except for the year Dan's son was killed in the Pacific. Except for that, we didn't miss a year. I just wish we had another sixty. We were close, closer than brothers, close as your two hands."

The Dragon at the Gate

Although men's friendships *can* be intimate and fulfilling, they often are not. Just as the fear of dependence inhibits intimacy between a man and a woman, the fear of homosexuality can inhibit intimacy between men.

If some men are ambivalent about the possibility of sexual intimacy in relationships with women, most men are terrified by the possibility of sexual intimacy in relationships with men. "[T]he fear of being taken for a homosexual," writes Stuart Miller in *Men and Friendship,* "or, worse, becoming one, is a main factor keeping adult men from close friendships."

Because of the profound anxiety they feel about homosexuality, many men reject other forms of closeness in male-male relationships. When two males touch, it's usually with exaggerated roughness: a slap on the back, a firmly gripped hand, a sharp jab on the shoulder. Contact should be brief and hard—best if it hurts just a little. Anything that smells of tenderness, anything unclenched or sustained, is suspect. To be gentle is to equivocate. Expressions of affection are brief, controlled, and rare. Except in extraordinary circumstances, the word *love* is forbidden.

"Kisses, tears, and embraces are not in themselves evidence of homosexuality," said C. S. Lewis in condemning the barriers that exist between men. "The implications would be, if nothing else, too comic. Hrothgar embracing

Beowulf, Johnson embracing Boswell (a pretty flagrantly het-erosexual couple) and all those hairy old toughs of centurions in Tacitus clinging to one another and begging for last kisses when the legion was broken . . . all pansies? If you can be-lieve that you can believe anything." Nevertheless, "it has actually become necessary in our time, to rebut the theory that every firm and serious friendship is really homosexual."

"The spectre of homosexuality," writes Don Clark, an expert on male encounter groups, "seems to be the dragon at the gate-way to self-awareness, understanding, and ac-ceptance of male-male needs." Clark cites a frequent com-ment among men who participate in his group sessions: "I avoid my feelings about other men because I'm afraid they might have something to do with homosexuality. I need the friendship of other men but I don't know how to find what I need from them."

"Honey, We're Home"

One kind of intimacy that men can enjoy without fear is the intimacy between men in groups. From bowling clubs to softball teams, from fraternal organizations to Thursday-night poker games, boys' night out gives men something that they can't seem to find elsewhere. Haunted neither by the ghosts of mothers nor by fears of impotence, the relationship between a man and his group is as close as some men come to real intimacy.

To relieve their loneliness, says Dr. Theodore Isaac Rubin, men "turn to continuing group association. They join a multitude of clubs, societies, organizations, fraternities, and orders. In groups, they find a well-defined hierarchy that lets them know in no uncertain terms precisely where they stand in relation to those around them. Groups particularly allow men . . . who have not had intimate relations with other men, a form of nonthreatening interaction."

In male groups—from football teams to VFW lodges, in the office during the week, at the corner bar after work, in exclusive men's clubs and pickup basketball games—many men can find the companionship of other men free from the implications of forbidden sexuality. "Men feel more comfortable in groups of men than one-on-one with another man," Dr. Alexander Levay told us, "because in groups any feared implication of homosexuality is dispersed."

Searching for the emotional intimacy they think can be found in male friendships, nurturing fantasies based on *Butch Cassidy and the Sundance Kid* and beer commercials, some men wander bars, bowling alleys, locker rooms, and poker games in search of emotional fulfillment. Although they often find companionship, they seldom find real emotional intimacy. "Male bonding is not a vehicle for male-male relationships," writes Dr. Joseph H. Pleck, "but rather is a substitute for them." Not being alone is as close as most men come to not being lonely.

Although they may satisfy a man's superficial need for camaraderie, groups can be hostile toward individuality. Members of a group rarely have a rounded sense of the other members as individuals, each with a unique set of problems, fears, feelings, and hopes. The result is that communication and intimacy are discouraged, and the primary functions of emotional intimacy—sharing and support—are cut off.

The bond between men in groups is often limited physically as well as emotionally. Just as two male friends rarely meet at either's home but instead at some neutral site like a gym, a clubhouse, or a bar, a man's place in his group rarely extends beyond the concrete limitations of the group. Studies of men in groups reveal that groups are seldom mobile: they are defined by the place in which they convene. Thus, a regular meeting at a bar after work seldom transfers to a weekend get-together at a member's house.

Women and Male Friendship

Some women worry that they are missing the magic, the special intimacy with their man, that they think exists in relationships between men. A girl who searches for conversation with her boyfriend on Saturday night wonders why he's never at a loss for words with his fraternity buddies. A woman who waits in frustration for her husband to put down the paper and look at her across the table can't help but wonder if she's being left out of the active life he seems to enjoy with a friend at the office, in the club, or on the team.

Recent psychological studies, however, indicate that most men now find it easier to open up and share emotional intimacy with women than with other men. "The modern male," writes Dr. Pleck, "prefers the company of women. Women rather than men are experienced as the primary validators of masculinity." In the course of interviewing men for *The Hazards of Being Male,* Dr. Herb Goldberg found that "almost all [of the married men] indicated that their wives were their only close friends, the only person they really trusted."

A major study of male college students by Dr. Mirra Komarovsky found that men are more likely to reveal their feelings to female friends than to male friends. Her results were replicated in a study at Oberlin College in which the majority of male students listed women as their primary confidants. "Women who think that men's friendships with other men are somehow better than their relationships with women," says a Washington, D.C., psychiatrist, "simply don't know enough about friendships between men."

Far from threatening a woman's relationship with a man, the presence in his life of a strong relationship with another man can reinforce and enrich his capacity for intimacy. Most women are aware that their own close same-sex friendships add to, rather than subtract from, their relationships with men. A woman who has a history of friendships with other women has cultivated a habit of intimacy, an emotional dowry that she brings to all her relationships with men.

A man's male friendships can make the same contribution to his capacity for intimacy. "Well-founded and self-caring, meaningful change and growth for men," says Goldberg, "can only happen if they develop same-sex support systems that would lighten their dependency on women and would also allow them to go through whatever changes they need to go through without fear of alienating their sole source of intimacy."

Men's friendships with other men serve a special function in a man's life, reinforcing his sense of self and sexual identity. They do not seek to exclude women, or take away their unique place in a man's life.

Manspeak

How Men Communicate

TO **MANY WOMEN,** men speak a foreign language: a language of few words, slight inflections, and little or no emotion; a language without intensity, or color—a combination of Humphrey Bogart's simmering monotone and Gary Cooper's "yeps" and "nopes." "When someone asked Gary Cooper to 'be there at high noon,'" laughs a woman in Los Angeles, "he just said, 'Yep.' If he was a woman, he would have said, 'What should I bring?' or 'Who else will be there?'"

We call this language Manspeak. Part English, part code, and part sign language, Manspeak is as closed as the men who speak it. Almost every woman has confronted Manspeak at some time in her life. First with her father, later with a boyfriend, a husband, a boss, an employee or fellow worker, and finally, perhaps, with a son, every woman has tried to communicate with an uncommunicative man. Many have given up in frustration. "Talking with a man," said a woman rancher in Oklahoma, "is like trying to saddle a cow. You work like hell, but what's the point?"

Manspeak versus Womanspeak

For most men, conversation isn't an art—it's a competitive sport. Women frequently complain that many men simply don't know how to sustain a conversation without trying to prove something. "When I talk with my husband—no, scratch that—when I talk *to* my husband, there are only two ways for the conversation to go," one woman told us. "Either it turns into an argument or it turns into nothing. Within a minute of asking him a question, he's either erupting or he's completely dormant. Everything in between is no-man's-land."

Because male conversation is so often competitive, men tend to see other participants as adversaries. Writing in *Ms.* magazine, Barbara Ehrenreich, author of *The Flight from Commitment,* called discourse among men a "sport, in which points are scored with decisive finger jabs and conclusive table poundings, while adversaries are blocked with shoulder thrusts or tackled with sudden interruptions."

As part of their general goal-orientation, men tend to think that conversation, like everything else, should have an objective to make it worthwhile. Words cannot merely be, they must *do.* Drs. Eric Skjei and Richard Rabkin, authors of *The Male Ordeal,* argue that when men talk, it's almost always to change someone else's ideas or actions. Without that goal, talk is idle and impotent. "Simple emotional ventilation," say Skjei and Rabkin, "regardless of its effects, tends to be seen as self-indulgent by [men]." When men talk, therefore, they usually invent a specific agenda: something to say to someone specific, even when all they really want is companionship.

Men have a variety of ways of taking control in a conversation. For example, they will talk only if talking is their idea. Women who try to initiate conversations often feel, as one woman told us, "like a matador coercing a bull." That feeling was documented in a study by sociologist Pamela Fishman, who "eavesdropped" on men and women in their homes. She found that when a man initiated a conversation, there was a 96 percent chance the subject would take hold and develop into a full-fledged discussion. When a woman initiated a conversation, there was only a 36 percent chance that anything would come of it. The man would seldom make any effort to participate.

Dr. Barbara Lusk Forisha conducted a study of class participation by male and female college students. Even in classes that were 66 percent female, male students controlled 75 percent of class discussions (based on the number of initiated responses). Forisha's findings support a 1974 study by Warren Farrell, who found that in mixed groups of six or more, "one, men generally speak most of the time; two, the conversation is centered on topics of interest to men; three, women tend to smile and ask questions of the men; and four, men tend to interrupt more often and in less supportive ways."

Men Interrupt More. One of the most common ways in which men control conversations is by interrupting. Both Farrell and Fishman found that the few conversations successfully initiated by women were often quickly redirected by interruptions from men who wished to turn them to subjects they found more agreeable.

Two California sociologists, Candace West and Donald Zimmerman, studied the conversational patterns of college students, focusing especially on the number of times men and women interrupted each other. Not surprisingly, their study found that men make significantly more interruptions than women, that men interrupt women more often than they interrupt other men, that interruptions by men are more likely to change the direction of conversations, and that men usually ignore interruptions by women.

From these and other studies, Barbara Ehrenreich concludes that women are "engaged in a more or less solitary battle to keep the conversational ball rolling. Women nurture infant conversations—throwing out little hookers like 'you know?' in order to enlist some help from their companions. Meanwhile, the men are often working at cross-purposes, dousing conversations with 'ummms,' non sequiturs, and unaccountable pauses."

The difference between Manspeak and Womanspeak isn't necessarily that men are less aware of people and their feelings, or even less adept at interpreting them than women. The real difference is that they have other priorities: controlling and ultimately winning. "This competitiveness," writes one commentator, "feeds the most basic obstacle to openness . . . the inability to admit to being vulnerable. Real men, we learn early, are not supposed to have doubts, hopes, and ambitions which may not be realized, things they don't (or even especially do) like about themselves, fears and disappointments."

What most men don't realize is that there are no real winners in competitive conversation. Only debates can be won or lost; only in debates is the purpose to compare the skills of the adversaries. Genuine conversations are partnerships involving cooperation and accommodation leading to surprise, delight, and, at their best, mutual revelation.

Facts, Not Feelings

Manspeak is a language of facts. From the specifications of a new car, to the earned-run average of a favorite pitcher, to the details of a sexual exploit, most men's conversations are focused on the quantifiable, the verifiable, the definite—rarely on anything as elusive as an emotion.

Men's magazines, in contrast to women's magazines, emphasize information, not analysis; results, not reasons. "Male problems are the last thing men want to hear about," says a female editor at *Penthouse*. "Men won't read anything negative about themselves. They just don't want to think about themselves that way. They want to see themselves jetting around town, buying the best of everything, with a pretty girl admiring them."

Instead of problem-related how-to articles, which fill the pages of women's magazines, men's magazines stress performance—sexual, business, sports. "The fiction," observes Dr. Joyce Brothers, "is characterized by action and adventure. . . . The nonfiction rarely treats such topics as male insecurities, health problems, relationships with colleagues at work, feelings toward women, dissatisfactions with the quality of life, roles as fathers and sons. There is little introspection in these magazines."

There is little introspection in many men's lives, either. Manspeak's emphasis on facts makes discussing feelings and emotions—the stuff of introspection—more difficult. "You can trace the degree to which two people are becoming intimate," says Dr. Loy McGinnis, a marriage counselor, "by watching how their talk moves from factual information to intimate revelation. Generally, new acquaintances restrict their conversation to facts; but as they know each other better, they begin to trust each other with opinions; finally, if they have become genuine friends, emotions will emerge."

This transition from facts to feelings is harder for men to make than for women because Manspeak has no vocabulary for intimate revelations. Therefore, most men, unlike most women, remain unschooled and insecure in the language of emotions. Facts become convenient insulation from both their own and other people's problems. While feelings are messy and elusive, facts are neat and manageable.

Although men do have bursts of intuition, irrational urges, and emotional reactions, they are taught not to trust them. Clark Byse, a contracts professor at Harvard Law School who referred to female students as "Mr." for years after they were first admitted, says he detests the word "feel." "I don't care how you feel," he tells students. "I'm interested in your brain, not your stomach."

Caught between the need to speak only in facts and the need to express their feelings, most men struggle to squeeze a square peg into a round hole. A woman who worked in the advertising division at Procter & Gamble's headquarters in Cincinnati told us about her former boss. "He was an incredibly creative man with a talent for sniffing out marketing trends. It was purely intuitive. But he always felt obliged to come up with a rational justification. Once when we were bringing out a new lemon-scented dishwashing liquid, I pressed him on why he thought it would go and he said, 'A *Wall Street Journal* study says women respond to yellow,' but he was going on his gut instinct. He was just afraid to say so. He didn't think an emotional decision was legitimate."

When a man gets into the habit of hiding his emotions behind a facade of facts, he runs the risk of developing an exaggerated and unjustified reliance on facts, even in situations where feelings are more important. In fact, a man will often grow more coldly rational and concentrate more single-mindedly on facts, the more his emotions are in turmoil.

Facts, of course, have their place in solving emotional problems, but by overemphasizing their importance, men avoid coming to grips with the ultimate reality of emotional disputes: feelings. Said one woman, "He tries to make me feel foolish because I can't sit and calmly discuss our problems like two lawyers. But he's the one who's foolish. Who can sit and talk rationally when the most important relationship in your life is on the line? I think a lot of men use that as a defense mechanism."

Sports and Sex

Work-related topics dominate men's conversations. Talking about work fulfills both the need to be goal-oriented and the urge to be factual. Underneath the objectivity, of course, many work-related conversations are also fiercely competitive. But when men aren't talking about work, their favorite topics of conversation are usually sports and sex. While conversation over the dinner table may falter, the dialogue in front of the TV set on Sunday afternoons never stops.

Almost invariably, when men gather with other men informally, the conversation hovers around these two subjects. There may be occasional detours—brief allusions to absent companions, questions about family, appropriate expressions of sympathy or anger, even an occasional political exchange. But for many men, less time is spent talking about sales figures, building schedules, or court agendas than about the game last weekend, the game next weekend, the game at the end of the season, and the prospects for next year.

Just as men's preoccupation with sports abates somewhat as they grow older, their discussions of sex become more tactful and "adult." Among grown men, the focus of sex banter moves away from the wildly fictionalized tales of sexual success (and excess) that are common in adolescence. No one believes them any longer and the dearth of individual accomplishments becomes something of an embarrassment. Instead, the conversation tends to focus on individual inadequacies, women's anatomies, and, most commonly, on safely impersonal jokes about "impotence, whores, homo's, and penis size."

The Style Gap

According to linguistics experts Dr. Lillian Glass of the University of California at San Diego and Dr. Robin Lakeoff of UC Berkeley, linguistic differences between men and women exist in both the style and the substance of their conversations. These differences, found in cultures throughout the world, result in frequent breakdowns in communication between the sexes.

For example, the Chiquito women of Bolivia are forbidden to use the masculine gender form of words such as *god, spirit,* and *man.* The women of certain Siberian tribes are required to pronounce words differently from men, and a man who uses the wrong pronunciation is considered effeminate. Japanese women are taught to avoid the use of masculine participles and verbs.

In America the differences are usually more subtle and transmitted more informally, but the speaking styles of the sexes still differ considerably. Where Manspeak is even and unemotional, the language of women is an Alpine landscape of emphasis and emotion. As Mary Helen Dohan, a former professor at Tulane University, points out, "Women tend to speak in italics: 'I just can't *believe* it! Are you *serious?* They are so *young.*'" This characteristic of Womanspeak has been captured in the prose style developed by *Cosmopolitan* editor Helen Gurley Brown.

In choosing words, women are more likely to reach for the extremes. While a man is *angry,* a woman is *outraged* or *indignant.* A man may think a book is *great* where a woman thinks it's *marvelous.* Women also pepper their conversation with what Dohan calls "intensifiers," especially the disembodied *so,* as in "This book is *so* good." Without a complementary clause ("so good that . . ."), the only purpose of *so* is to convey conviction. The same phenomenon occurs in French, German, Danish, Russian, and other languages. "When the *so* itself becomes the italicized word ('She is *so* mean!')," says Dohan, "the modified term becomes even stronger; the meanness is beyond description."

In Manspeak, by contrast, emphasis and intensity are avoided. Taught to remain "in control" even when they talk, most men speak in a monotone, relying for emphasis only on pauses, the masculinity of the words used, and casual profanity—rare in women's speech. Where a woman would say, "It's *such* a nuisance," a man would say, "It's a damn nuisance."

Women in many cultures also tend to undercut their statements with questioning tags. For example, "It's a good book, don't you think?" Just as Japanese women frequently conclude their sentences with the deferential phrase *kashira* (meaning "I wonder"), an English-speaking woman will add, "isn't it?" And if she doesn't add a deferential question explicitly, she'll add it implicitly, by the tone of her voice, transforming a direct statement into a diplomatic inquiry. Men, on the other hand, tend to compensate for tentativeness with exaggerated certainty: "God, it's a great book."

Finally, where men are competitive in their speech, women tend to be cooperative. Instead of giving commands, a woman is more likely to make requests: "Would you hand me that book, please?" instead of "Hand me that book." "When a woman wants something," says Dr. Lillian Glass, "she tends to use tones and words that add up to a request. She therefore expects others to phrase requests in the same sort of language." When they don't, says Dohan, a woman's "psycholinguistic expectations" are frustrated, and "resentment simmers."

The Art of Indirection

Manspeak has a certain *Alice in Wonderland* quality to it. Not only are men's conversations mined with interruptions, non sequiturs, and "unaccountable pauses," they are mazes of blind alleys, misleading comments, and false clues. Especially when they're trying to express feelings, most men neither say what they mean nor mean what they say. In Manspeak, the relationship between words and meanings is turned topsy-turvy.

"I asked my husband why he'd been moping around the house for a week," a high-school teacher in Grenada, Mississippi, told us. "He said, 'The neighbor's cat died.' A few days later he was still moping, so I asked him again. He said, 'My stomach's acting up.' Two days go by, he's still moping, so I ask him again, 'What's the problem?' This time he says, 'The grass needs mowing.'

"All this time I knew what it was. He was upset because I was going to the state teachers' convention in Jackson—he hates to see me go. It happens every year the same, but he'll never come out and say anything."

Why do men resist expressing themselves directly? Why do some men choose to hint at love rather than come right out and say, "I love you"? Many men express themselves indirectly as a way of protecting themselves. Indirection allows a man to test a woman's feelings without revealing his own, to see if she will lower her guard before he lowers his, to assess her vulnerability without surrendering his own.

Indirection is a toe in the water; it saves a man from a fate worse than freezing: rejection. If a man says something to a woman directly, he invites a direct response; honesty invites honesty. If he tells her that she has made him unhappy, he may hear that she doesn't care. If he says, "I love you," he may get silence in return. A direct statement of emotion is a gamble, which some men aren't willing to take. An indirect statement, on the other hand, leaves the speaker in control. If the response isn't the one he seeks, he can claim—also indirectly, by a laugh or a puzzled look—that she has misunderstood what he said. Nothing ventured, nothing lost.

Some men who are afraid to reveal their feelings resort to teasing and joking. "It serves as a barrier and false front," says Dr. Theodore Isaac Rubin, "which helps them avoid the need to reveal true emotions. Through the use of teasing, men can displace affection as well as hostility. Teenage boys rely on this tactic with friends they like, just as adult men too often utilize it to establish contact with children."

The language of teasing and joking is a world of trick mirrors, in which almost everything means something, but something other than what it appears to mean: a world in which a man's most difficult or serious feelings are most likely to surface in the guise of humor.

Because of work commitments, Terry had been separated from his fiancée for a year. He was clearly insecure about Debbie's fidelity and tried to shield himself from potential hurt by finding little time for phone calls or correspondence, and none for visits to see her. Terry would never have admitted his worries directly, yet they consumed him night and day.

The only way he found to express his anxieties was through joking. At lunch in the company cafeteria, he would lean back and muse aloud: "I wonder who Debbie's going to be with tonight." He would describe Debbie's sexual appetite and torture himself with speculation as to her current adventures. It was easy to see through his bravado, as it often is with men who are driven to express their deepest fears in the clown suit of humor.

The Problem with "I Love You"

Why is it so hard for men to say "I love you"? In the catalog of complaints about closed men, there is no more insistent question. Other symptoms of emotional repression are tolerable; but those three little words possess a magic for most women that makes their absence almost unbearable. For many women, opening up *means* being able to say "I love you."

But when confronted with the demand for "I love you," many men balk. They feel they've expressed their love in hundreds of ways—in daily gestures, in routine comments said with a special emphasis. They complain that women burden these "three little words" with too much emotional baggage; that, ultimately, the feeling is more important than the phrase.

Between most men, love can be expressed only by using the devices of indirection and subtlety allowed under the rules of Manspeak. It can be cloaked in a factual statement ("You're the best friend a guy could have"), hidden in a pledge of support ("You can count on me"), mentioned indirectly ("I want you to be there"), or buried in a joke ("Why do I put up with you?"). It may come as a clap on the back, a laugh, or just a look that says, "You and I are the only two sane people in the world."

"It's not that men don't express affection," says a male college professor in Austin, Texas. "It's just that the way they express it is not experienced as an expression by most women. We will express our affection for other men by slapping them on the back, or telling a dirty joke, or raising our voices. It's a rare sight to see a man express his love for another man. It happens only in movies—and even there it's pretty rare. A guy has to be dying."

Unfortunately, the same rules apply to men's feelings

toward women. They use the same circumlocutions, the same indirections, the same subtle gestures. From "they're playing our song" to "I think I'll trade her in for a new one," men insist on expressing their love in a language most women don't know. As Merle Shain suggests, even "Is dinner ready?" can mask grand passions.

Mixed Signals

"It was nice meeting someone so
sensitive, aware, and vulnerable.
Too bad you're such a wimp."
Real Men Don't Eat Quiche

OF ALL THE forces that keep men closed—childhood indoctrination, the culture of manhood, the fear of dependence, ungiving fathers, unfulfilling friendships, even the language they speak—the final and perhaps most important force is women themselves. This was undoubtedly the most startling truth that emerged from our research: very often women don't *really* want men to open up. In a world of changing sex roles, some women are now affected by the same forces that cause men to fear intimacy. As a result, they themselves may come to fear intimacy and respond warily to men who offer it.

Women who choose closed men, especially very closed men, don't do so by accident. The same cultural factors that make men closed also make women want closed men. "Because women are influenced by the same stereotypes as men," says Dr. Alan Stone, "many of them are sexually attracted to men who are aloof and unknowable. It is part of what turns them on sexually. To the extent that men read these mixed messages, there is obviously a conflict between what women say they want and what they really want."

All too often, the very women who urge men to be open

and conciliatory in their relationships want them to remain closed and aggressive in their careers. Despite the complaints, the concern, and the calls for open men, many women are trapped by the same stereotypes that imprison men. They feel vaguely cheated when the cowboy who won their hearts with a steady gaze and choice words unexpectedly exposes a soft heart filled with unromantic anxieties.

Many women, at the first sign of trouble, will throw romance to the winds. Partly because most women have traditionally relied so heavily on men for their economic and emotional support, the first sign of anxiety, doubt, or weakness may be seen as a threat. In many relationships, a man with a problem is like a boat with a leak. Sometimes a woman's first thought isn't that the boat needs repair, but that she might drown.

Most women insist that they want men who express vulnerability, shed tears, and show affection. Yet, both at the movies and in real life, they are drawn to men who respond to "I need you" with a strong hand, and "I love you" with a silent stare. In fact, many women want a man to be strong and silent one minute, warm and emotional the next. They want men to be vulnerable *and* invincible. When they need excitement, they long for mystery and lament men's weaknesses; when they need support, they demand warmth and decry men's reticence. The closed man is both a frustration and an enduring fascination. He is both the unresponsive, inaccessible man who refuses to share his feelings or give emotional support *and* the shadowy romantic male who lurks in many women's fantasies.

A woman named Sarah acknowledged that women sometimes help keep men closed. "Some women obviously want closed men," she told us. "I don't necessarily think that every woman is really all that fond of so-called open discussion, of revealing vulnerability. If she's the kind of woman who wants to depend on a man, then she doesn't want a man to be vulnerable. What she wants is the kind of considerate behavior from a man that proves she can depend on him; she doesn't want the kind of vulnerability that true openness reveals. After all, everyone is vulnerable.

"I think people get into trouble when they have a specific role they have to play. Luckily, I escaped that kind of role. I never looked upon men as my rescuers or my salvation. I didn't require that every man I got involved with be a rock I could rest on—that he be the whole basis for my existence.

"If you want a man to be the center of your life, as women seemed to fifty years ago and some women still do, then it's pretty damn important that the guy be perfect—that he not be vulnerable, that he not spill out a lot of problems, that he actually be this big daddy who's going to make everything be all right."

Inevitably, these seeming contradictions leave most men even more uncertain and insecure about what it means to be a man. Do they respond to a woman's pleas for emotional openness and intimacy or to the subtle signals that "silence is sexy"? If they struggle to maintain the illusion of invincibility, will a woman leave in search of a "best friend"? If they beat down their male pride and reveal their vulnerability, will they lose out to the irresistible allure of a strong, silent man? Faced with the confusion of many women's expectations, many men never leave the shelter of emotional isolation, where, even if nothing is gained, at least nothing is lost.

Women should be able to sympathize with the dilemma of the closed man; all too many of them face the same contradictory expectations from men. The sex kitten of a man's fantasies has to be able to transform herself into the mother of his memories: a sultry mistress by night and a conscientious homemaker by day. He expects the impossible no less than a woman who wants a vulnerable stud and a mysterious friend.

We spoke to one man, a thirty-six-year-old divorced former Marine Corps officer, who admitted that his wife had tried to help him confront his feelings before their split and that he had tried to cooperate but felt confused. "I really felt in a bind in this emotional-vulnerability area," he said. "After all, she always liked the fact that I was a Marine. I understand that a lot of men want a woman to be a Florence Nightingale with her kids and a whore in bed. They want her to be everything. I think women have got a legitimate gripe. But they don't see that they put men in the same bind. They want a man to be vulnerable when they want him to be vulnerable, and strong when they want him to be strong. We've got a gripe too."

Part Two:

Overcoming Men's Fear of Intimacy

Leading a Man to Intimacy

Woman as Friend

THERE IS A cure for the Ulysses Syndrome, for the man who will not let himself respond emotionally, but it requires that at least one person in the relationship have the courage to make it happen. In relationships with closed men, that person is almost always a woman. "A woman has to *lead* a man into intimacy," says Dr. Ari Kiev. "In most relationships, she's the one who's in touch with her feelings, she's the one who understands, she's the one who really has to take the lead."

Why does a woman have to shoulder the burden of making the relationship work? Why can't a man help himself? "As a rule, it won't work that way," says Kiev. "He's usually too dumb when it comes to emotions. He doesn't know how. He doesn't know what he feels or what he wants. He's paralyzed by his fears—the fear of rejection, the fear of dependence, the fear that he's not the man he ought to be. He needs help."

A woman must ask herself whether she truly wants to make the commitment to help a man change. However much she may want to, she cannot alter the circumstances of a man's past, nor can she completely shield him from the pressures of social conformity. But she *can* alter the present and shield him from pressures within their relationship. To do so, she will find that she too is called upon to change in various ways.

She must ask herself whether she really wants intimacy. She must ask herself what she has done or is doing to prevent her man from communicating his feelings openly. Is she giving off signals, consciously or unconsciously, that she *doesn't* want him to open up? Does she want him, perhaps without even knowing it, to remain strong and silent? When he is open, does she behave in ways that reward him for it, or in ways that close him down again? Is she afraid that she won't love the man inside as much as the man she has learned to live with? Is she afraid that a change in their relationship will demand more intimacy and openness than *she* is willing to give?

If she's sure that she does want a more open relationship, the first thing a woman should do is convince her man to want one too. She should help him see that, far more than aloofness and competitiveness, emotional fulfillment is vital to his psychological and physical well-being. "It's important to let a man know," says New York psychotherapist Cese MacDonald, "that, although he may have been denying them, his feelings have always been there, that he was born with them just as a woman was born with them, and that the culture may have denied him the freedom to express them. He doesn't have to remain closed, but in the end only he has the power to choose for himself the possibility of freely expressing his feelings without feeling his dominant role threatened."

MacDonald is correct, no doubt, in saying that in the end only a man has the power to open up. But a woman can do much to lead him in the right direction.

Independent and Giving

How can a woman provide this kind of support, especially if a man resists her approach as a threat to his independence? We heard many women complain that men rebuffed their efforts to help because they saw them as attempts at manipulation. "If I put my foot down and demand to know what's bothering him," said a Wisconsin woman married for eleven years, "he thinks I'm attacking him. If I smile benignly and cook his favorite dinner, he thinks I'm being manipulative. Either way, he retreats."

According to Dr. Kiev and other experts, there is a way for a woman to move closer to a man without triggering his fear of dependence, or seeming dependent herself. "You have to combine two opposites," says Dr. Kiev. "You have to be both independent and giving. People think those are contradictory, but they're not—*if* you're independent and giving in the right ways. Instead, most women react to a closed man by being dependent and demanding."

Many men find dependent and demanding behavior unattractive. One woman we spoke to remembers a lover saying to her, "Everything you say sounds midway between a whine and an order." That kind of behavior, relying as it does on the power of guilt and coercion, throws up a red flag for many men, and the flag says, "Manipulation."

Many women think they are "giving" if they're constantly available and never offer a moment's difficulty or disagreement. They subordinate their lives and egos to their husbands or lovers and consider it a sacrifice for love. "Many women grow up with the notion that men are all-powerful and that women have to learn the 'Cinderella game,' " says Dr. Kiev. "They feel they always have to be attractive and adaptive so that men won't hurt them, so that men won't reject them. Ironically, they put men on a pedestal and consider that supportive."

In fact, this kind of subordination almost inevitably leads to a buildup of resentment. On the one hand, a man sees it as fundamentally dependent behavior and feels the implicit pressure to reciprocate. His emotional-detachment defense mechanisms are triggered and he moves out of reach. On the other hand, the woman is often angered by the man's inability to respond to her sacrifice with a commensurate degree of affection—one that many men find difficult to muster—and her anger only distances him further.

The other mistake women often make is to demonstrate their independence by being demanding. "Sometimes I feel that getting angry and calling him on the carpet is the only dignified way out," says a thirty-four-year-old woman in North Carolina. "I have needs too, and I have to say them straight out in a loud voice because I know he'll never ask." Whatever the validity of such claims—and men can learn to recognize them—men generally react negatively to demands from women, especially if they're made in a belligerent or emotional state.

Blowing up may have cathartic benefits for a woman, but it's not the way to open up a man to the possibilities of intimacy. "A woman should also resist the temptation to be 'bossy,' " says Dr. Kiev, "even if a man encourages or tolerates her bossiness. Almost all boys learn to tune out their mothers when they're being bossy, so they learn to tune out their wives too. It's a passive-aggressive maneuver that becomes an important part of a man's defenses against intimacy."

What does it mean to be independent and giving in the day-to-day business of a relationship? It means to have the emotional independence to *let* him be distant when he's in a bad mood (even if she's in a bad mood too), to let him complain when he's had a hard day (even if she's had a hard day too), and to let him have moments of privacy (because she needs them too).

It means fighting the tendency to revert to dependent or demanding behavior when the level of his emotional giving falls below the level of her emotional need. One woman may have to correct for her inclination to endow men with too much power and subordinate herself into a position of dependence. Another may have to correct for her inclination to become demanding when she wants to assert her independence. It means that a woman must distance herself from her man's problems instead of seeing his struggling as a rejection of her. Instead of seeing him as an all-powerful person who is depriving her, she must see him as a flawed individual, like herself, who needs her strength and her tenderness.

By being independent and giving instead of dependent and demanding, a woman can subdue the fear of dependency that keeps a man at arm's length emotionally. She can be the one to whom he comes for respite from the demands of masculinity and independence. She can be the woman who, at the same time, gives him rest and sets him free.

"By being dependent and demanding," says Kiev, "a woman *invites* a man to withdraw emotionally. The moment she becomes independent, elusive, and mysterious, a man will climb mountains to go after her."

Stages in a Relationship with a Closed Man

Because women, as well as men, bring to relationships their own complicated histories, doubts, and anxieties, the effort to make a meaningful connection can be complicated and frustrating. Many relationships resemble a Marx Brothers movie in which the characters chase each other through a labyrinth of doors. Each time one enters, another exists. One exits here but enters there, another is suddenly caught alone with all the doors closed. People cross each other's paths, stumble over each other, catch disappearing glimpses, then disappear themselves.

Despite the confusion, the closed man's relationships, controlled as they are by the fear of dependence, do tend to follow a simple pattern: attraction, withdrawal, and stalemate. For a woman who finds herself caught in this pattern, understanding how it works and why is an important step toward breaking out of it.

Stage One: Attraction. When a relationship is new, a man plays a role consistent with his ideals of masculinity. The behavioral stereotypes are comfortably clear and uncomplicated. Often, the woman plays the role of mistress while he plays the suitor, the conqueror, engaged in a test of his male prowess. Like a rooster, he struts his colors in an attempt to attract a female. The woman becomes for him a prize which, in the winning, bolsters his masculine self-esteem.

Of course, "winning" a woman involves more than a show of feathers or sexual potency. Winning her may at times require a show of affection, indications of openness, and a willingness to give emotionally when called upon. In this first stage of a relationship, even a closed man is on good behavior and can produce almost any kind of emotional response in the service of his ultimate goal. He can allow himself a level of vulnerability and intimacy that, later in a relationship, would cause inner turmoil.

Women often complain about men seeming open and communicative during courtship but then becoming silent and withdrawn when the relationship has settled into a routine. "Most men are so frustrating," we were told by a divorced woman in Washington, D.C. "They hold out all sorts of promise, and then, just when you tell yourself, 'This is one I can trust,' they pull out of reach."

In the early stage of a relationship, the closed man permits himself a rare openness, the opportunity to express his need for intimacy, a need normally precluded by the masculine stereotype. "Compelled by his intense desire for intimate and lasting sexual involvement with a woman," say Eric Skjei and Richard Rabkin, "a man may at first be delighted to find himself involved in the stable, captivating relationship he has longed for. But the very fulfillment of long-standing and insistent desires for sexual acceptance and gratification can evoke deep-seated fears of becoming too open, too vulnerable, and the risk of painful depression should the relationship fail."

Thus, in the first stage of a relationship, even a closed man is capable of intimacy, but it's usually an intimacy based on his notions of male success, not on his acceptance of his own emotional needs. Outwardly, he may appear open, but inwardly, he is gradually withdrawing from the intimacy implied by his actions.

At this point in a relationship, chronically detached men may either take up with another woman simultaneously, or bolt the relationship altogether. "Terrified of becoming engulfed," says Dr. Theodore Isaac Rubin, "detached men make a fetish of freedom." These are the men who suffer from an advanced and accelerated form of the Ulysses Syndrome, who refuse to commit themselves to a single woman even for a short time, for fear that they will become too dependent.

But for most men, the attraction of intimacy is too strong to abandon so early. They stay in the relationship, but withdraw psychologically, widening the gap between their apparent commitment and their inner reservations. "The trouble," says Michael Korda, "is that while most [men] passionately want and seek intimacy, at the same time we *fear* it. Intimacy involves commitment and choice, a closing off of other possibilities, the decision that this one is for keeps. You give up certain freedoms, and you run the risk of failing, with all its emotional fallout." Unfortunately, the closer many men get to intimacy, the stronger their fear becomes, the more the Ulysses in them cries out for distance and self-protection.

Sensitively attuned to a man's responses, a woman usually perceives his emotional withdrawal. The result, typically, is a request for reassurance: some insistence, subtle at first, that the gap be closed, that the man stop holding himself back from real commitment. The man reads this as a demand.

Stage Two: Withdrawal. Ironically, the withdrawal stage often follows some outward sign of commitment—typically, moving in together or marriage. The man may feel suddenly trapped, when, in fact, the public commitment has really just brought to the surface anxieties and fears that had not yet coalesced into felt emotions.

A forty-year-old divorced saleswoman in Washington, D.C., explained to us why she refuses to marry her boyfriend of five years: "I know that the minute I do, no more courtship, no more flowers, no more attention. The shoe will be on the other foot. *I'll* be the one who'll have to give *him* attention. I'll become his mother, the way I was with my first husband."

At the point of commitment, a man may react with hostility and resentment, reactions that often mask his fear of dependence. It is his potential dependence on her that he fears and resents, not her dependence on him. The relationship "is suffocated by the heavy weight of his dependence and draining demandingness," says Dr. Herb Goldberg. "If she abandons him, his emotional lifeline will have been cut." In characteristic fashion, a man responds to this threat by activating the self-protective mechanism of emotional detachment that he learned as a child. "He detaches himself," says Goldberg, "with occasional moments of explosiveness, to control the torrent of unexpected feelings."

Although a woman may fear being suffocated in a relationship as much as a man (especially in light of the recent cultural emphasis on breaking the traditional pattern of subordination to men), she "can deal with these feelings far more easily than a man for whom dependence is automatically equated with weakness," says Dr. Rubin. Also, she is probably not conditioned, as most men are, to express her fear as resentment. She is more likely to turn her anger on herself, or even to blame herself for the man's feelings of resentment. Unfortunately, guilt, like dependence, is ultimately a demanding emotion and is often perceived by a man not as guilt, but as a further demand for support.

The transition from attraction to withdrawal may be marked by the transition of the woman's role from mistress to mother. On an unconscious level, many man desire this transformation and bend all their relationships with women toward it. "For a son," a woman in New York told us, " his mother, no matter how old, is always the most beautiful woman in the world." Given this bond, it's hardly surprising that a man, after leaving his mother's embrace, would attempt to transform her successor into a replacement. A woman, for reasons of her own, may be drawn willingly into the mother role or even attracted to it. Yet this role tends to discourage emotional honesty. A man's feelings for his mother may be profound, but they're not conducive to intimacy.

Although he wants to salvage his threatened independence, a man also continues to need his woman's approval. He needs to vindicate her maternal love, to be her "good little boy." Understandably, he is loath to share with her anything that jeopardizes that image, anything that might reflect badly on him and tarnish his "mother's" affection with reproof. Instead of coming to his wife as an adult for emotional give-and-take, the man comes to her as a child comes to his mother, seeking her protection and support.

In most relationships, of course, the reasons for a man's emotional reticence are seldom exposed. A woman who is the victim of the resentment and hostility that mark the second stage of a closed relationship can seldom see beneath them to the fear of dependence that they mask. If a man "never clearly defines what it is that he needs or wants from a woman," concludes Dr. Goldberg, "she will in turn either come to hate him for it or 'suffer through it' masochistically."

Stage Three: Stalemate. In this stage, the relationship slips into a pattern of mutual withdrawal and emotional distance. The portrait of the closed man that most women paint is taken from this stage. He is sullen, isolated, moody without explanation, given to long periods of silence and sudden, unexplained outbursts of emotion. A man finds a release from the fear of dependence in this behavior pattern. "Sulking," says Dr. Rubin, "represents withdrawal—and that in itself represents a form of freedom and lack of involvement."

A man in stalemate resists sharing even major emotional problems such as job insecurity, death, illness, or impotence.

But most significantly, he resists any attempt to discuss his own behavior and the problems that it creates for his relationships. He becomes a stranger in his own house. "Of all the areas in which men fail women," say Drs. Skjei and Rabkin, "this is the one that cuts the deepest and, ultimately, evokes the most contempt. Nothing contrasts more sharply with the masculine image of self-confidence, rationality, and control. . . . This, more than anything else, disillusions women about their men."

Breaking Free

To break free from the pattern of fear and withdrawal that controls many relationships, a woman must add the role of friend to her roles of mistress and mother. When a woman is a man's friend, she can override a man's protective mechanisms and establish an intimate relationship immune from approach-avoidance inner conflict.

Friend is also the only role in which a woman doesn't see a distorted view of a man's personality. To the mistress of the attraction stage, a man must play the lover. To the mother of the withdrawal stage, he must always be the perfect son. Only to a friend can a man open up entirely without fearing dependence or the loss of his masculinity. "The most successful marriages are those in which the spouses are best friends," says Dr. Josef H. Weissberg, professor of psychiatry at Columbia University. "They start out sexually attracted to one another, but stability comes with friendship."

The steps required to achieve this kind of friendship differ depending on what stage the relationship is in. But, no matter how advanced the estrangement, no matter how ingrained the current roles, almost any relationship, with commitment and love, can be remade into a friendship that provides both sexual and emotional fulfillment.

Breaking Out of the Attraction Stage. Often in the first stage of a relationship, the primary source of inner conflict for a closed man is sex. As both a proving ground for his masculinity and an invitation to intimacy, sex becomes the focus of his fears of dependence. The best, if not the easiest, way to avoid triggering the emotional-detachment reaction that often accompanies sex is to avoid it at the start.

"Sex has a tendency to accelerate a relationship," a marital therapist in Houston told us. "People find themselves jumping into bed, doing the most intimate human acts with someone they really barely know. It's hardly surprising that all sorts of defense alarms go off in both men and women. The old way, when sex was the natural and beautiful culmination of the long process of getting to know someone intimately, had its advantages."

"The double standard hasn't really changed for men," Dr. Kiev told us. "They're taking advantage of the changed morality to satisfy their own needs. So a woman will tell herself she really has to sleep with a man, because if she doesn't sleep with him, he's going to go find someone else. I say, fine if you want to sleep with him, go right ahead, but if you want to build a relationship, that's a separate issue."

If a man and woman wait until they have some depth of shared emotional experiences, the approach-avoidance conflict aroused by sexual activity is substantially reduced. Delaying sex allows a man to deal with his need for emotional intimacy before becoming involved in the often more difficult subconscious battle to prove his masculinity in sex. By allowing him to resolve his inner conflicts one at a time, a woman makes it more likely that he can resolve them in favor of intimacy.

"Relationships seem to have worked better before the sexual revolution," writes Michael Korda. "Our parents, certainly our grandparents, planned for the long haul. They were married or engaged before they went to bed with each other. They assumed (admittedly not always correctly) that marriage would last a lifetime, and they accepted that true intimacy was a product of habit, the gradual breakdown of the barriers people form to protect their egos, the sharing of life experience."

In past eras, formal courtships and year-long engagements set a grace period during which a man and woman could learn about each other and develop mutual trust. By the time they faced the challenge of sex, they were already good friends. Too often in the age of sexual liberation, the language of trust is learned too late—or not learned at all. Both men and women pay the price in missed intimacy, brief relationships, and failed marriages.

Breaking Out of the Withdrawal Stage. One sign that premature sexual intimacy may have triggered defensive detachment mechanisms in a man is the falling off of sexual attraction. "At this point," says therapist Cese MacDonald, "the couple should simply acknowledge that the sexual attraction has fallen off, or better yet, that there has been a transformation. They need to accept the fact that life is a roller coaster, in or out of bed, and in or out of a relationship."

The purpose of accepting changes in the sexual chemistry is to counteract a man's natural tendency to withdraw from a relationship in which he fears the limitation of his freedom. When the cream of infatuation has been skimmed from a relationship, both a man and a woman may begin to engage in recrimination and self-recrimination: "Is it my fault he doesn't love me anymore?" "Is it my fault she doesn't find me attractive anymore?" Questions like these tend to undermine a man's sexual confidence and put his masculinity on the line. Feeling jeopardized, he is more likely to withdraw than give more. By directing his attention away from the fault-finding process and toward positive solutions, a woman can prevent further withdrawal.

During the withdrawal stage of a relationship, a man and woman often forget how to read each other's signals. When people in a relationship hurt each other, instead of trying to communicate their feelings, they try to protect themselves from further hurt. The result can be a breakdown in communication.

"In one typical situation," said Dr. Kiev, "the sexual relationship breaks down. The husband thinks his wife is angry with him so he never really makes an advance. Then she complains that he's not sexually aggressive enough. Then he tries, very tentatively, to touch her. He puts his hand over hers. But it comes off like a request for therapy —very unromantic—and she's turned off. He should say, 'I really want to sleep with you tonight,' but he's afraid that she's going to reject him, because she's done it before, so he doesn't."

To repair this kind of breakdown in communication, both people have to realize that they're giving out the wrong signals, that they're not communicating their real feelings or what they really want from each other. "Each person takes what the other is saying far too literally," Dr. Kiev told us. "Instead, they should recognize the behavioral impact of communication."

According to the experts, what two people say often isn't as important as how they say it. What one says to the other triggers off a response, which in turn leads to a response, which triggers off yet another response. It follows a certain kind of pattern, so that today's argument about dinner has the same structural characteristics as yesterday's argument about the rent. To really listen to each other, two people should try to discern the pattern of their exchanges as well as their substance.

Once a couple begins to perceive and understand this pattern, they can begin to stand back and try to change it. "You almost have to be able to see yourselves like two characters in a long-running play who are reading the same dialogue over and over and over again, year in and year out," said Dr. Kiev. "Once you see it, all of a sudden, you have some control over your communication, because you begin to be more aware.

"What I often suggest to my patients is, 'Think of yourselves as being together in the same canoe. When you start escalating the argument, you're both standing up in the canoe and you're both going to fall in the water together.' When that realization sinks in, most people start thinking less about themselves and more about the canoe." Only when a man and a woman both realize that the relationship has needs of its own, independent of their individual needs, can they begin to see how it benefits both of them and how much of a stake they have in preserving it.

Breaking Out of the Stalemate Stage. When a relationship reaches stalemate, it's usually because a couple has refused to deal openly with their problems. The result of this neglect is often a gradual falling off, a long period of estrangement, and then a letting go. The husband goes his way, the wife goes hers. The patterns of hostility, resentment, or indifference are allowed to develop undisturbed, and the more entrenched they become, the more difficult it is to break their hold on a relationship.

For some couples, even after years of stalemate, the prospect of getting to know each other again is exciting. "Sometimes the relationship has been put on hold not because two people are incompatible, but just because they've gone their separate ways," Dr. Kiev told us. "Traditionally, he goes off to a career, she gets involved in raising the kids. But the spark that ignited the relationship in the first place is still there, just waiting for a little attention to rekindle it. Getting to know each other again can be truly exciting for those people, like reliving the honeymoon."

For others, however, the road to rejuvenating a relationship may not be so easy. How hard that road is depends largely on how much is left to salvage, how much remains of trust. "A couple who wants to reestablish communication after a long silence—and that can be a few days or a few decades—must look for whatever common threads they have," says Cese MacDonald. "That's where they should start the rebuilding process."

In the absence of a common ground on which to begin rebuilding intimacy, the strain on an already uncommunicative relationship becomes most severe. "For couples without a focus of common concern," Dr. Robert Garfield told us, "a marriage can become extremely stressful." In such cases, many experts suggest a partial separation. For most couples, of course, even those with a severe intimacy problem, taking up separate residences, however briefly, is an unacceptably radical step. Instead, many couples try a partial separation within the context of their relationship.

These couples work to develop time apart from each other—small separate vacations, more evenings with separate friends. If one partner is not working, the separation is an opportunity to find a job, full time or part time, paid or volunteer, that can grow into an alternate support system. Developing a new personality outside the home or the office can help both people achieve a greater sense of self-sufficiency, and at the same time enhance a man's sense of independence. As he feels more independent, he will fear dependence less.

This kind of separation can help give a couple the clearer perspective they need to confront their problems, retract their defenses, put hostility behind them, and begin to rebuild a relationship based on the kind of trust and acceptance of dependence that are necessary for genuine intimacy.

According to Dr. Kiev, a couple should "put their lives on separate tracks—parallel but separate. Each person on his or her own track." Too often, couples confuse spending time together with intimacy. Many couples, Kiev told us, make the mistake of merging their lives, of doing everything together. If the woman eats dinner before the man gets home, he throws a tantrum. So she always waits to eat until he's there. And if she's not hungry, she sits there while he's eating. They never take a vacation separately. "They never do anything separately," said Kiev. "If he wants to go fishing, she gives him a sour look, so he doesn't have the freedom to go."

In other relationships, the problem is just the opposite. Instead of the woman refusing to allow the man to be independent, he refuses to allow *her* independence. "The man is too patriarchal, too domineering. He doesn't really acknowledge the woman as a real person. He doesn't recognize the validity of her point of view. For her part, she plays the Cinderella, masochistic, complementary role. In that case, she needs to become more independent and he needs to become a little more supportive of her independence."

It doesn't take years of marriage for these problems to develop. Whether the stalemate is the result of two months or twenty-five years of missed communication, the issues are the same: the need to be independent; the need to listen to each other; the need to really appreciate the "differentness," the uniqueness, of the other person; the need to tune in to the other person and to be helpful. The more helpful you are, the more help comes back.

Having It All

What all the expert advice adds up to is this: the best way to overcome a man's fear of dependence, at any stage in a relationship, is to bring friendship into the relationship— friendship not in the "buddy-buddy" superficial sense, but in the deeper sense of undemanding, independent support.

Bringing friendship into a relationship, however, doesn't have to mean ushering sex out. Friendship is the answer, but not friendship instead of sex. In fact, a close friendship is essential to maintaining the quality of a sexual relationship. The point is that if you put friendship *first*, the other pieces of a relationship, including sex, will fall into place. "After the heat of a sexual infatuation has diminished," says Dr. Avodah K. Offit, "the ability to be affectionate often determines whether the sexual attraction will last."

When sexual intimacy and emotional intimacy are allowed to enhance each other, the result is a relationship that includes friendship but is more expansive and more profound than friendship—the kind of total relationship that's also known as love.

Unlocking the Intimate Man

The Basics

INSIDE EVERY CLOSED man is an intimate man waiting to be reached. This inner man wants to be freed, but needs someone else to make the first move, to extend a hand, to unlock the door of masculine stereotypes and dispel the fears of dependence that keep him closed. Some women are better at this than others. They have the gift of caring and empathy— in short, friendliness—that makes unlocking the intimate man seem easy. Among the most successful of these women we know is Janice.

Janice is a writer and magazine editor with the bones and the swagger of Katharine Hepburn. Whether she's busy in her San Francisco office or at home in the Berkeley loft she shares with Craig, Jan is a running lesson in the fine art of communication. Alternately eager with questions and rapt with interest, she makes every conversation seem easy and inevitable. To the accompaniment of thoughtful questions and sympathetic noises, she makes everyone around her feel energized and enlightened.

To be with Jan and Craig together is a pleasure and a privilege. They carry with them an air of lighthearted good nature, warmth, and concern. Of the two, Jan is more open and animated, constantly expressing her feelings—even when they happen to be jealousy, dislike, or anger—but always attentive to the feelings of others. Of course, there are times when she arrives alone at a dinner party, upset because Craig is still working, and complains that Craig is uncommunicative. But as soon as he arrives, they come together in a single presence that is alive and feeling. Things were not always so.

When Janice met Craig, he was a designer in the art department of her magazine. A tall and slender but still boyish man with warm brown eyes, Craig found wordless satisfaction in the designer's visual world. "Craig was married then," Janice recalls, "but I always thought he was *so* sexy. And I used to tell him so." Seven years later, long after Craig had left the magazine, they ran into each other on the street.

They chatted for a while, but Jan had to go on to an appointment, *"Call* me," she said. "She sounded like she really meant it," remembers Craig, "so I did." Later on, Jan reminisces, "Craig would ask me to say '*call* me' the way I'd said it that day."

The early stage of their relationship was charged with intensity. Chattering with excitement, Jan hardly noticed that she was doing all the talking. "I always just couldn't wait to go to bed," she says. Soon she moved into Craig's loft. But after the initial flush of courtship, communication became a major problem. "He stopped listening to me," Jan says. "He wasn't interested, and I was just devastated."

When they sat down to dinner at the black slate table in their white-tiled dining area, Jan would start a conversation and Craig would just stare out the window, watching the sailboats on the Bay. "Dinnertimes were real showstoppers," Jan recalls. "I'd sit down at the table and try to talk with him about something and he would be totally somewhere else."

One night Jan raised the subject of Craig's unwillingness to express himself. His response: "What do you want to hear? Noise? You want to hear noise at dinnertime? Is that what you need?" Jan's outburst was immediate, "I hate you," she said, "I'm leaving." Jan didn't leave, but that incident was the first in a long series of fights. "It got to the point where I almost preferred the silence," says Jan.

By now Jan was using all the communication skills she could muster. Gradually, Jan found out where Craig's silences came from. "In my family, talking was pretty much guaranteed to get some criticism," says Craig. "Not the talking itself, but what was said. My father was so critical— not just about what we said but about what we did. He generally treated my brother and me as if we really couldn't do anything competently." Says Jan: "In a way, Craig was repeating that kind of behavior—being real remote."

The first breakthrough for Jan and Craig came as the result of a problem. Despite the powerful mutual attraction they felt, it was taking them awhile to work out their sex life. "I wasn't used to telling a man what made me feel good sexually," Jan says. "I expected it to happen without talking about it. It bothered me that sex wasn't as good as it had usually been for me, and I thought it was because Craig was inexperienced. I told him so."

One night Craig came home with a copy of a book called *Frigid Women*. His therapist, a woman, had given it to him to give to Jan. "That book was the turning point for me," she says. "I knew I wasn't frigid—I mean, the book was about women who *never* had orgasms—but I realized I wasn't getting something across. But it had seemed weird to me to talk to Craig about what he could do, because I thought he should know."

The need to communicate about sex and the fact that Jan had to be more self-revealing brought them closer, but they remained caught in the same pattern of attraction and withdrawal. Jan recalls: "We'd get real close—up to a point —and then Craig would start to get uncomfortable and withdraw, and then I'd get mad and say, 'I'm leaving.' "

Craig says: "When she told me she was leaving I felt it

as a rejection of my whole being. I couldn't see it as her still loving me but not liking my behavior." But Jan's threat to leave did make Craig realize that he wanted her, and that he wanted to be more like her. "I had felt something was missing in my life," he recalls. "There were a couple of times when it got real rough, when I felt if I wasn't able to make some changes then I would lose her."

Craig had been seeing a therapist since the breakup of his first marriage, and when their troubles continued Jan suggested they see someone together. "If we hadn't," she says today, "I'm not sure we would be married." The couple went to a family therapist. To Jan's surprise, Craig didn't respond to the therapist, either, when she asked him questions. "It helped me to see somebody deal with this and not go off the deep end. And then I also began to understand that Craig's silences weren't directed at me. They were the result of something he felt about *himself*."

Therapy helped both Craig and Jan change their behavior. "I learned not to fly off the handle," Jan says. Gradually, Craig learned to be more open and giving. "I found out how to talk about myself, what was happening to me, and how I felt about what was happening. I also learned how to listen. Sometimes it still seems like work to me—when I'm tied up with work, thinking about a lot of other things. It should be as easy as stepping into a shower, but when I'm preoccupied it's difficult for me, whereas Jan is always ready to listen—which seems amazing to me." A year ago, convinced that they would achieve the intimacy they wanted, Jan and Craig decided to get married.

"One of the most satisfying things to me now," Jan says, "is when I realize I haven't said, 'What are you thinking?' for a couple of weeks. I haven't had to. And when Craig sees me frowning or looking puzzled and he says to me, 'Well, aren't you going to tell me?' The shoe feels much better on the other foot."

When we asked Jan and Craig what had enabled them to break the communications barrier in their relationship, Jan told us very much the same thing the experts told us: "I began to see that being independent and not demanding, being *friendly,* was the only way. I could give, because I was raised to give, but it was difficult not to be demanding. I felt I was giving and not getting anything back. What helped was when I began to understand that Craig wasn't withholding things from me because he didn't want me to know them but because of his own needs. Realizing that his silence wasn't a rejection of me made it easier for me to be less demanding."

Craig says: "The withholding person has to want to do it—open up. If the other person is demanding, the feeling is that he has to do it for *her,* and that can only end in resentment. He has to feel he's doing it for himself. If she's demanding, he's going to feel like it's work, like it's a problem.

"When Jan got angry, I would feel bad at first and then realize how important she was to me, and I would want to make up. At that point, she was at a safe distance, so I could then start to move closer. But it definitely didn't help for her to get that angry or threaten to leave. If you're going to open up to someone else, there has to be trust. If you're under the gun of somebody walking out, it's hard to be trusting. It would have had the same effect if she had just said, 'Look what you're doing to yourself.' "

See the Problem from His Perspective

The first step in helping a man to open up is to understand why he's closed. For Jan, the revelation came when she first met Craig's father and saw how his constant criticism had driven Craig into his shell. "It's important to try to understand why these feelings are too awkward to communicate," Dr. Josef H. Weissberg told us, "and to understand the history of how these feelings came to be too awkward to communicate. You must understand where this awkwardness came from and begin to deal with that very rapidly."

This can be more difficult than it sounds because men are often very adept at concealing their problems. But Dr.

Alan J. Wabrek, director of medical sexology at Hartford Hospital in Connecticut, underscores the importance of understanding: "A crucial ingredient for a good marriage is understanding your partner's perspective. Everyone sees the world through different eyes. When partners view issues differently, they can easily become polarized, unless they make an effort to see what the other person is seeing."

If a woman begins to see a man's insecurities from his perspective, she will better appreciate the difficulties of opening up in the face of those insecurities. Janet Wolfe, Ph.D., told us that men who won't open up are usually kept from it by "anxiety or anger. If the problem is anxiety, he's probably telling himself that if he reveals himself to you, he'll *lose* himself. He'll lose his identity. If the problem is anger, he might be thinking, 'She's constantly asking me to express my feelings. It's terrible that she's doing this, and she's a terrible person for doing it.' "

These are not rational explanations, which is the point. Part of the solution is to bring the irrational explanations to the surface and get the man to defend them. Will he really lose himself if he shares himself? How will he be less of a person? Are you really such a terrible person for wanting him to open up? Understanding how he is reacting to your requests for emotional openness will help him begin to answer them.

But a woman must also understand her own needs. To any relationship, both the man and the woman bring expectations that have less to do with the relationship than with their respective childhoods. Jan eventually realized that Craig's silences reminded her of times in her childhood when her father would become depressed and not speak to anyone in the family for a week at a time. The irrational intensity of her anger had its source in these painful childhood experiences.

Dr. Alexander B. Taylor told us, "In childhood, important relationships are formed that often are not adequately resolved. As a result, later on in life you may expect your spouse to behave like someone in your past. You might think, for instance, 'He reacts to me just as my father reacted to me.' "

Therefore, before a woman can understand a man she has to understand herself. She has to free him from *her* past, and stop trying to use an existing relationship to resolve the problems left unsolved by an earlier one. "You have to see your partner as a different person with his own identity," concludes Taylor. "To do this, you must know *yourself* well."

Set the Right Example

One of the most important steps a woman can take to help a man open up is to set the right example. "Women," says a psychologist, "have to apply to themselves the same lesson they're trying to teach men: that in opening up, in showing vulnerability, a person has to brave the risk of rejection." Early in their relationship, Jan was called upon to be open with Craig on the vulnerable subject of sex. Exposing herself, she was able to advance their closeness. If a woman is comfortable with her own emotions and expresses them easily, she's proof that it can be done.

Dr. Albert Ellis, the well-known behavioral psychologist, tells of having been opened up by a woman who knew how to express her emotions easily. "I went with a woman who was a genius at love," said Ellis in his Manhattan office. "When she wanted a man to do something—to express himself, to send presents or flowers, to write poems, or whatever—she was simply a marvelous model. She didn't ask *him* to do it. She just did it for him in a highly enthusiastic manner *herself*. I'm sure she trained a number of men to be the way she liked them because she was so enthusiastically that way herself."

Marriage counselor Loy McGinnis offers similar advice to women. "The best policy," he says, "is to be as transparent as possible yourself. Then your partner is likely to respond by opening up in a way he has undoubtedly longed to do, perhaps for years."

Candor begets candor. Be honest with a man, and

chances are he'll learn to be honest with you. But candor doesn't always justify saying the first thing that comes to mind. It is always important, even in the closest and strongest relationships, to strike a balance between candor and consideration. Dr. Laura Singer says, "Although honesty is an ideal, to be honest at *all* times is really to act out a lot of aggression and hostility. You have to consider what the impact of what is said will be upon your lover or husband."

Think through what you're going to say, don't just say the first thing that comes to mind—it may be more hurtful than helpful. Elaine Killian, a marriage and family counselor in Long Beach, California, says, "Many of us have gone from being overly timid about sharing feelings to thinking we must spew out all of our negative emotions. Just burdening someone with 'I feel this' or 'I feel that' is unhelpful or self-indulgent. Before you can communicate effectively, you must understand why you're upset."

Let Him Feel for Himself

Sometimes a woman inadvertently keeps a man closed by assuming all of the emotional "duties" herself. "Very often," says therapist Cese MacDonald, "where the male has given up expressing emotions, the female will take over as if to compensate for his failure to express them. She'll give out twice as much. That can be overwhelming and even frightening to a man. I am not saying that the woman should repress her feelings, just that she should be careful not to co-opt his."

Often, men are willing accomplices in this transfer of emotional responsibility. In order to distance himself in a relationship, a man will reject emotions altogether. By looking to the woman for all emotional responses, he implicitly denies that he has any such responses himself. Many women take this deference as a token of intimacy, however meager, and assume the role eagerly, gradually becoming the couple's exclusive emotional mouthpiece, at parties, in family discussions, and with friends.

One way to prevent such a lopsided arrangement from developing is for the woman to temper her emotions so as not to overwhelm and frighten the man. By refusing to be automatically responsible for emotional behavior, the woman sends a nonthreatening signal: "It's your turn to show some emotion," instead of "I demand that you show some emotion."

Many women are raised to think that they're responsible for men's feelings, says Dr. Robert Garfield. "Everyone is caught in their own role. Women often feel that it's their job to be the nurturers and the caretakers for the man because he can't do it for himself." It's not surprising, says Garfield, that we have a stereotype of "the stoic man," who in moments of crisis "will turn to his wife and expect her to cry or at least be upset.

"When I work with couples I really try to make the man responsible for his own feelings. What this says to the woman is, you don't *have* to be responsible for him. He's capable of expressing the entire range of feelings all by himself. Many women are delighted to hear it.

"If you ask men to be accountable for themselves," says Dr. Garfield, "you'll discover that they can do it—not only *can* they do it, but they're really pleased and relieved to do it." After putting his advice into practice, women often return to Dr. Garfield and say, "I never thought he'd be so interested," or "He talked more than he has in twenty years." "It's partly because the woman previously assumed that he *couldn't* talk, so she talked for him, and he assumed that he didn't have to talk, so he didn't bother."

Don't Force the Issue

A man whose fear of intimacy flows from deep-rooted insecurities can't be forced to open up. Any effort to pry him open will only trigger a defensive reaction. He'll only feel more insecure about his inability to satisfy your needs within the relationship.

Dr. Hal Arkowitz, professor of psychology at Arizona

State University, explained to us that "the most important thing to avoid is letting your efforts to open him up turn into a power struggle. Often, what happens is that the more a woman wants it, the less he wants her to have it. He wants to give it to her on his own, which means not giving it."

Again, a woman should avoid being demanding. The solution, Arkowitz suggests, is to make your complaints known without demanding that he respond to them. "The woman has to let up a little on trying to make him open up, but not on communicating her desire that he open up. There's a fine line between the two." She has to convince him that if he opens up he'll still be desirable, that he can be both vulnerable and exciting, both dependent and masculine. "You've got to let him know," one woman told us, "that it's okay if he doesn't win all the time. You've got to let him know, you've got to *convince* him, that he's even sexier when he's vulnerable."

Many women make the mistake of trying to overcome a man's resistance to showing emotion by convincing him that it's *good* for him to show emotion. That's simply not enough incentive. A man has to be convinced that it's more than good, it's *appealing*.

A man's life can be changed if he really comes to believe that he's loved *because* of his ability to show emotion. A case in point is a man we know named Stan. Like many men, Stan thought his girlfriend, Joan, loved him because he was a real man, because he was a good lover, because he had a good job, and because she needed his love. It's a heavy burden to think you must live up to someone who thinks you're flawless, who thinks you're "some kind of a god," and for Stan that burden was becoming increasingly difficult. Their relationship was in the doldrums.

One day Joan sat him down and they had a long talk, during which all of her complaints came pouring out. "I found out a lot that day," says Stan. "I found out that Joan knows now—and always did—that men are *not* gods. That other men *are* more godlike than I. There *are* better lovers. I *am* a shit. She does *not* need me. But she *does* love me.

"I had three fears: that I was vulnerable, that Joan would find out I was vulnerable, and that she'd leave me because I was vulnerable. That day, all but one of my fears was realized. The earth didn't stop. I didn't walk into a black hole. In fact, I felt liberated, and we decided to live together."

Build on Trust

Of all the elements that contribute to an open, intimate relationship, the final, essential one is trust. If a man can't trust a woman, it's unlikely that he will ever be able to open up to her. "Trust, for me, is the key to intimacy," Dr. Lewis Long told us. "In the best of relationships, you can tell a partner, 'I hate you sometimes,' or 'I'm leaving for three days until we cool off,' and know that things *will* cool off."

Trust is confidence in your relationship and confidence in your partner. It doesn't come easily, and it's never complete, but relationships can't function without it.

How to Talk to a Man

Techniques for Better Communication

TO ACHIEVE INTIMACY, a man and a woman have to find a mutual language that both can understand, a language for expressing feelings and resolving problems. There are three ways a woman can help develop this common language. First, she can teach a man, by example and by encouragement, some key lessons about the language of emotions. Second, she can learn to listen more closely to the sometimes muted and indirect ways in which men express their feelings. Finally, she can try to accept and understand the value of nonverbal as well as verbal forms of communication.

Teach Him the Language of Emotions

A vocabulary of intimacy can emerge only if both people in a relationship help it along. "There is a male and female code of expression," says one psychiatrist, "and you have to know how to translate feelings and ideas into each other's language. In an ideal world it would be different, but in the world as it is today, it's not very likely that a man will go out on his own and learn the female code of expression. A woman's going to have to come to him. If she wants a full measure of emotional dialogue, *she's* going to have to make the effort and teach him her language."

Find Common Ground. Many women operate on the basis of a false assumption about intimacy. Intimacy, they believe, consists only in sharing feelings. They equate intimacy with "love talk." Thus, they try to solve emotional problems in a relationship by talking about their feelings for each other, formulating them, dissecting them, criticizing them. Because such discussions are relatively common during the initial, infatuation period of most relationships, many women continue to believe that they are the most definitive proof of emotional commitment.

But this initial, self-sustaining phase in a relationship seldom lasts. Only unrequited love can live on itself indefinitely, and when it does, the result is obsession, not intimacy. Once this phase passes, a relationship needs to be sustained by shared experience. A woman who wants her man to talk to her must make sure they have something to talk about. "What brings men closer to each other—or to women for that matter—is above all shared action and shared experiences," says William Novak in *The Great American Man Shortage.* "Shared humanity is generally not enough. Women, by contrast, are more likely to want to share their feelings before shared action occurs.

"For example, two women friends who meet for dinner might begin their conversation by telling each other how they are feeling. In a similar position, two men might begin with stories of their work, and only later, if at all, will they discuss their feelings. For women, then, the key question is 'How *are* you?' For men, it's more likely to be 'How are you doing?' Or 'What have you been up to?' "

In other words, men often find it easier to base a relationship on interests outside the bounds of the relationship itself. An inexpressive man typically finds it easier to disguise personal sentiments in the seemingly impersonal. The emotional give-and-take in a group of men watching a football game is only the most boisterous example of how men are willing and able to establish intimacy by sharing their feelings about some common shared interest.

A woman can take advantage of this willingness to get a man in the habit of discussing his feelings. Instead of talking about football, they can talk about a movie, a book, newspaper headlines, or J.R.'s latest plot on "Dallas." Starting with this kind of nonthreatening emotional dialogue, a woman can gradually bring the focus of sharing closer to a man's own inner life. In addition, along the way, a man learns some of the vocabulary of intimacy, as well as the habit of exploring his own feelings.

Teach Him How to Express Himself. When two people begin to talk about their feelings about each other, or especially about their emotional problems in a relationship, they need to know how to express themselves clearly. As a rule, women are more practiced than men both in understanding their feelings and in articulating them. Therefore, a woman may have to teach a man the skills necessary to express himself.

Many therapists recommend that a woman encourage a man to use the "I" exercises devised by sex experts Masters and Johnson. In a conversation, each person simply begins his or her sentences with "I": "I want . . ." "I think . . ." "I feel . . ." This process, usually easier for women than men, trains them to be in touch with their emotions. "To communicate your feelings," says Dr. Alexander Levay, "is to stop the blaming and start the process of trying to understand what the other person is saying."

Other experts point out that for this process to work, the couple should specifically agree beforehand that they will never express agreement or disagreement about what is said; that the sole purpose of the conversation is to understand. "A couple that wants to communicate," says Dr. Alexander B. Taylor, "has to know how to talk without searching for ultimate truth or consensus."

The point is for men to learn to distinguish things they think and things they feel. As soon as a man can make that distinction (one more familiar to women), he can begin to understand his motivations. He can begin to ask himself why he's reacting in a particular way, what in his past makes him afraid to express his affection, why he wants to direct the conversation away from himself. "The trick," says one psychologist, "is to get him communicating with himself. Once you do that, he can start communicating with other people."

Be Specific. "Most men tend to be very task-oriented," says Dr. Taylor. "They tend to be bottom-line-oriented—they want to solve issues." A woman can take advantage of this common male trait by asking direct questions and presenting specific problems with specific solutions.

Jim, an investment banker in Boston, agrees that the best way to handle a man is to give him a specific problem to be solved, rather than a general one to be analyzed. "Most men don't think of being closed as a problem, so they see no need to discuss it. For most men, a problem is defined as something that needs to be solved. By that definition, being closed is not a problem. Having your wife come to you with problems A, B, and C is much easier to deal with."

"Don't talk about how things are and what you don't like about them," says Dr. Marcha R. Ortiz, a supervisor at the Family Therapy Institute in Washington, D.C. "Talk instead about how you would like things to be. Conversation that dwells on the problems leaves them at that level. The interaction is so negative that it perpetuates itself."

Instead of suggesting a long conversation about "our problems" and hoping that some intimacy develops along the way, a woman can often get a more revealing response if she asks a direct question about a difficult topic: What are his fondest memories of time spent with his father? What were his friends like when he was a child? How did he feel when he had sex for the first time?

Unlike most women, who regularly engage in personal

conversations, men are not generally accustomed to responding to intimate questions. Nor are they good at circumlocution. They're used to being asked straight questions about impersonal topics and giving straight answers. A straight question about a personal topic may just give you an equally straight answer.

Exchange Secrets. The token of intimacy that a man may be most willing to give is a secret. Because men seldom talk about personal matters and are seldom questioned about them, they are often a veritable treasure trove of intimate secrets aching to be told.

"I am fascinated with secrets," says a female marital therapist in Connecticut. "I think secrets do much to close people off. And we all have them. For example, feminists—and I consider myself a feminist—have a hard time letting anyone know that there are times when they just want to curl up with a man. If you keep that kind of thing secret from literally everyone, it weighs on you, and it has the effect of closing you off in other ways.

"I really think that if you can get someone to tell you their most important secrets, you've gone a long way toward creating an open relationship. What is the secret a man has carried his whole life? Has he always been ashamed of what his father did for a living? Has he always envied his brother or sister for getting more of his parents' affection? Did he do something terrible as a child? Whatever it is, persuading him to get it off his chest can be very important. To relieve a secret burden like that can change a life, reconstitute a personality.

"Basically, the way to get a man to think about telling you these kinds of things is to have the courage to tell him the secrets from your own past—and not the things you *want* him to know, the ones you don't want him to know. The ones you're embarrassed about." Only if you let a man know that you trust him with your complete past will he have the trust to give you his.

The Art of Listening

One of the best ways to help a man open up is to listen to him—really listen. Many people are busy formulating a response when they should be listening. "Listening requires attention and concentration," says a Minneapolis psychiatrist. "It's more important in intimate conversations than talking, because you need to give the speaker the confidence to continue."

"An important aspect of conversation is memory," says a female broadcast journalist in New York with a reputation for getting people to tell her things they won't tell anyone else. "Mention something a man said long ago, or even earlier in the same conversation—psychologists do this all the time. The fact that you didn't forget, that it seemed worth remembering, is very flattering and comforting.

"I get as much as I do out of people because I really want to know what they're going to say and I convey that interest all the time. I look straight at them, I don't waver once, and I make it clear that, at least at that moment, there is absolutely nothing in the world I would rather do than listen to him talk. Even with famous people, that doesn't happen to them very often, and they respond with honesty."

If that kind of concentrated attention happens to famous people rarely, it happens to most men hardly ever. Speaking with their male friends is more like a contest than a conversation, and all too often conversation with women is weighted down with masculine insecurities. By creating the right environment, by letting him know that she really wants to hear what he has to say, by really listening, a woman makes opening up easier.

Be Prepared for His Openness. One of the most common ways in which women unknowingly discourage emotional openness is by indicating that there are some unspecified things that she doesn't want to hear. A man's first strivings toward emotional intimacy should be reinforced, regardless of how awkward or even painful they may be. If a man has never opened up to his emotions before, his first emotional stirrings may surprise a woman more than they please her.

"One of the things that women frequently do when their mates become more self-disclosive," Janet Wolfe told us, "is to jump down their throats when they are. A woman I'm treating now said that the one thing she doesn't like about her husband is that he's emotionally constipated and doesn't really share feelings. He finally shared with her the fact that he had almost no sexual experience when he married her, that he was really excited by other women, and that he really didn't know quite how to deal with it. He didn't plan to *act* on those feelings in any way. They were just feelings he wanted to tell her about. But she responded with anger. She started screaming and yelling and carrying on. We talked about how she wasn't exactly rewarding him for being disclosive. Later she was able to respond in nonattacking ways and to be a better listener. As she continues to change, he's going to feel less terrified about opening up."

Therapist Cese MacDonald confirms Wolfe's advice: "A woman has to learn not to react with obvious anger if he says things she doesn't like. Usually there's some kind of benefit for her in not hearing what he has to say—that's why his silence has been maintained. If she truly wants him to open up and express his emotions," MacDonald told us, "she might have to give up that secondary gain, the benefit of not knowing what's going on in his head. She might not like it. She has to be prepared for that."

Another way in which women sometimes discourage the very openness they seek is by failing to treat his revelations with the necessary care. A woman named Susan, who described herself as "verbally promiscuous," confessed to us that when her friends came by, she would tell them anything and everything her husband had told her. "We'd have a deep discussion one night," Susan admitted, "and the next morning as soon as Jim was out the door I'd be on the phone, blabbing around details of his life that it had taken him years to feel secure enough to share with me. He's uneasy with many of the people we see, because they know his entire history."

A person doesn't have to reveal a confidence in order to abuse it. There are times in the course of any relationship when it's tempting to misuse sensitive revelations. The temptation is especially strong in moments of anger. "We were having a fight not too long ago," a woman in Atlanta told us. "I didn't feel like having sex, and he wanted it. He was so furious, he said something about my weight that really hurt. I was so mad, I reminded him of something he did to his sister when they were young. He had just told me about it, and it was an admission that had cost him a lot. He was so hurt he didn't even answer back. I never felt so terrible, and I know it set him back a long way."

Look Behind the Words. Part of the good listener's job is to look behind a person's words and behavior and try to understand what they mean. "You must learn how to listen," therapist Laura Singer tells her female clients. "All kinds of needless misunderstandings can be avoided by asking yourself, 'Where is he coming from?' 'What is he *really* trying to tell me?' "

Behind the facade of sports jargon and blue humor, for example, men are communicating more than most women realize. Sports talk, for example, is really more about people and feelings than about statistics. Men who watch football, baseball, basketball, or any sport, tend to "adopt" certain teams. Their spirits sink and rise with the team's. They single out certain players for special attention, like favored sons, and follow their careers intensely.

The pattern should be familiar to anyone who watches soap operas. In Anne Tyler's novel *Dinner at the Homesick Restaurant,* a seventy-year-old woman suddenly becomes obsessed with the Baltimore Orioles because "she viewed each game as a drama, fretted over the gossip . . . from the sports pages—players' injuries, rivalries, slumps, mournful tales of young rookies so nervous they flubbed their only chances."

Just as many people share in the trials of surrogate families on daytime and prime-time soaps, many men take pleasure in the added dimension of excitement and opportunity provided by sports. A man gets the same feelings of belonging and caring when he watches Monday Night Football that some women get watching "Dallas" or "General Hospital." In talking with other men about the game, he can share and prolong those feelings.

The fondness of many men for sex jokes and banter is also both less and more than it seems. In fact, these often have little or nothing to do with sex at all. Tales of sexual adventures, innuendos of inadequacy, paeans to the female anatomy, and off-color jokes are usually nothing more than filler: harmless banter to keep the conversation going, to maintain the lines of communication with other men.

In most cases, two men trading dirty jokes are no different from two businesswomen beginning a lunch with introductory remarks on each other's clothes. The significance of the conversation is not in what is said but in the pleasure of conversing, in the simple joys of sharing another person's presence. It's also a way to open a conversation, to smooth a first meeting, or to ease the transition to weightier matters. Sex talk is for many men what small talk is for many women: a form of caring.

Body Signals

Some relationships survive without the benefit of conversation by relying primarily on nonverbal communication. Many women we spoke to carried in their heads a glossary of a man's personal signals, both verbal and nonverbal. Using these signals, women can often decipher even the most cryptic message. One woman described with exasperation the decline of her marriage, which bottomed out in divorce. "It got to the point," she said, "where he used physical gestures instead of talking. He would put his finger on the back of his neck. That meant he had a headache—'Don't talk now.' I felt like Anne Bancroft in *The Miracle Worker,* trying to make him understand: L-O-V-E means love."

Listen to His Body. An important part of knowing a man is being able to read his body language. A man's body is often an eloquent intermediary, conveying in its own language the feelings a man can't express in words.

One night, a woman named Ronnie was talking with her husband, Charlie, as he stood next to the refrigerator with his legs crossed at the ankles and his arms across his chest. "His body language at that moment said he was totally closed," recalls Ronnie. "His body language said, 'I don't like what you're saying.'

"I said, 'Honey, you really don't like what I'm telling you, do you?' He said, 'What are you talking about?' I said, 'Look at yourself.' And he looked down at his legs and arms and laughed, and said, 'You're right.' Since then, I've paid much more attention to reading his body. Men say little enough as it is. You can't afford not to hear it when his body is screaming at you."

A woman who has learned to communicate physically can use that knowledge when verbal communication breaks down or, if a man is extremely closed, when verbal communications can't be established. "Sometimes," Ronnie told us, "when Charlie and I are having a fight or a disagreement, and things are going downhill fast, I'll just reach over and touch him. The whole conversation changes. We'll still talk about it, we'll still have a disagreement, but we won't be as angry with each other. It's hard to be nasty and horrible to someone, or even just cold, if they're hugging you or holding your hand."

Sometimes it isn't a man's body but his pattern of behavior that communicates his feelings. Beth, a young woman in St. Louis, tells of how her marriage took a sharp turn for the better when she finally learned to decode her husband's actions. "I used to wonder seriously if my husband hated me.

He'd come in the door after work, walk right by me and not say a thing, not even look at me, march up to the bedroom, and close the door. Half an hour later, he'd come out, just as friendly and charming. I'd be sitting there worrying and burning the meat loaf and thinking, 'Oh lord, what have I done, what have I done?' But he'd never say a word about it.

"It took me a while to figure out what was going on. I knew it wasn't problems at work. When he's got problems at work, he comes in ranting and raving and hungry, he kicks the refrigerator door, and he yells at the dog. When he comes in quiet and goes straight to the bedroom, it's the *traffic*. He had a bad time on the drive home, but he hasn't got anything in particular to yell about. So he goes back to the bedroom, and after a while he's okay.

"I learn something new like that almost every day now that I've got the hang of it. Just a few months ago, I figured out that if he calls from work, he wants me to be here when he comes home. So I make it a point now. He doesn't want to ask me straight out. He doesn't want it to seem like he's ordering me to be here—and I appreciate that. Now he doesn't have to."

Communicate with Sex. For many men, the most intense nonverbal communication occurs during sex. According to Dr. Robert Garfield, women need to understand that for many men in loving relationships sexual activity isn't a substitute for emotional expression—it *is* emotional expression. "With men," says Garfield, "there's often an enormous focus of emotion in sex. Often, emotions and sex are synonymous for men, but not for women. That's one of the big problems that keeps on coming up in therapy.

"You know the movie *Annie Hall*? In that film, a psychiatrist asks Woody Allen, 'How often do you have sex?' and he says, 'Hardly ever, three times a week.' Annie Hall answers the same question, 'All the time, three times a week.' That's partly because sex means different things to men and women."

Unlike women, who have a wide range of ways in which

they can communicate and feel close, men tend to compress the meaning of intimacy into the sex act. When they're deprived of that outlet, they become frustrated and upset because they're cut off from the only source of closeness that they know.

"Knowing how men view sex makes it a lot easier for women to deal with it when it comes up," says Dr. Garfield. "It's one way of breaking through the stereotype that all a man wants is to use a woman as an object. That's *not* all that men want. Men are really interested in intimacy and closeness—they just have different ways of defining it for themselves."

Say It Physically. A woman in Cleveland told us about how she uses body language to communicate with her husband: "Stroke him, touch him, hold his hand, rub his neck, knead his feet. I think touching is the best way to help anyone open up. Men like to think of themselves as exclusively sexual creatures, but they aren't all that different from women. They really need touching for strength as well as for sex."

Men already have a vocabulary of physical affection which consists primarily of exercise and sports-related contact. In the past, this vocabulary was usually not shared with women because any such contact generated sexual expectations. Ironically, women, too, have a vocabulary of physical affection. But they are usually cautious about sharing it with men because such moves might be misinterpreted as an invitation to sex.

Fortunately, the recent popularization of exercise regimens has brought these two languages closer together, allowing men and women to communicate physically without feeling trapped by sexual expectations. Jeff Aquilon and Nancy Donahue Aquilon, two of New York's top models and exercise buffs, have developed an entire exercise program around the concept that exercising together puts your relationship as well as your body in better condition.

If a man has trouble keeping sexual and nonsexual physical affection separate, the experts suggest that gentle reminders may be necessary. "You may want to take a roaming hand and hold and stroke it," counsels one expert, "or return an exploratory gesture with a robust hug, kiss on the cheek, and announce that you think it's time to put the peas on."

Whatever the solution, the point is the same. "Almost everybody responds to cuddling," Dr. Robert Whitaker told us. "Make some physical contact with him, any physical contact with him. Touching is more caring than 'I love you' for many people."

Ultimately, a man and a woman can't analyze, argue, or arrange their way to intimacy. Although they can create the right conditions for it, they can't make it happen. If two people learn to understand each other's feelings, however; if each partner reaches out and embraces the other partner's emotions and concerns; if each genuinely tries to learn the other's language, both verbal and nonverbal; they will have come a long way toward achieving the kind of closeness they both yearn for.

A Casebook
of Closed Men

THERE IS NO one "closed man." Depending on his personality and the circumstances of his life, a man who fears intimacy may evolve in a variety of ways. He may play the macho man, the charmer, the loner, the company man, the intellectual, the sensitive artist, the workaholic, or some variation on these basic roles in order to maintain a safe emotional distance, to keep the world at arm's length.

The particular personality of a closed man, however, will affect how a woman is best able to reach him. A man who is silent needs to be approached differently than a man who is glib; a man who has completely submerged his need for intimacy in a frenzy of activity presents a different challenge than a man who acknowledges his own sensitivity and vulnerability.

Because each case is different, there is no simple, unvarying formula for overcoming a man's fear of intimacy. A woman in Chicago asked us wistfully to provide a "treasure map" for her husband. "I know it's buried in there somewhere," she said. "Just tell me where to dig." Unfortunately, there are no easy routes, no treasure maps. Therefore, these cases do not constitute a textbook—they could never be comprehensive enough to embrace all varieties of people and problems. Instead, they serve as examples and reassurance: examples of how particular people confronted and solved their problems, and reassurance that others can do the same.

The Strong, Silent Man

The Direct Approach

"The strong, silent type." In many women's lives, the phrase has a unique, contradictory resonance. Although many women are still excited by its overtones of smoldering sexuality, many know only too well the frustrations of trying to create a bond of intimacy with a strong, silent man. "It's easy to *want* a strong, silent man," says one married women in her early forties. "Most women grow up trying to coax a smile out of Daddy. But once you *have* one, you wonder if the game's worth the candle."

Of all closed men, the strong, silent man is uniquely American. The qualities he represents—hard work, purposefulness, integrity, courage, and perseverance—were appropriate, even essential, to the pioneer culture of the earliest settlers. A century later, when the western frontier was opened, the same rules applied: self-reliance, social reserve, and emotional terseness were the male attributes of choice. Whether they were homesteaders or railroad barons, to the strong, silent men of the day went the spoils of the era.

Thanks to the modern media, these frontier values are still part of our culture. Movies and television have "frozen" cultural norms—especially sex roles—in the age of the Wild West. "The cowboy in motion pictures," says psychiatrist Alfred Auerbach, "has conveyed the image of the rugged 'he-man': strong, resilient, resourceful, capable of coping with overwhelming odds."

The Cowboy Syndrome

Drs. Jack O. Balswick and Charles W. Peek, authors of "The Inexpressive Male," have labeled the chronic inexpressiveness of the American male "the Cowboy Syndrome" and identified John Wayne as its prototype. Wayne, as he appears in the forties' westerns of Howard Hawks and John Ford, is a celluloid portrait of the strong, silent man, a lesson in being closed for generations of moviegoers. He's independent ("I'm startin' my own herd"); goal-oriented ("I'll kill any cowhand not good enough to finish what they start"); and controlled ("There's nothing I hate worse than a man who's soft").

Emotional reserve is a crucial part of the cowboy persona projected by Wayne. Emotions, especially the "soft" emotions, are considered unmanly. "Don't apologize, son," says Wayne to a young soldier in *She Wore a Yellow Ribbon*, "it's a sign of weakness." Unfortunately, this reserve extends even to intimate relationships. "The on-screen John Wayne," says writer William Manville, "doesn't feel comfortable around women. He does like them sometimes—God knows he's not *queer*. But at the right time, and in the right place—which he chooses. And always with his car/horse parked directly outside, in/on which he will ride away to more important business in Marlboro country."

The strong, silent man, like the cowboy, is not devoid of feelings; he simply can't express them. According to Balswick and Peek, the mark of the real man "as portrayed by Wayne in any one of his many type-cast roles . . . is that he does not show any tenderness or affection toward girls because his culturally acquired male image dictates that such a show of emotions would be distinctly unmanly."

Being manly, however, even in Wayne's world, doesn't require purging the heart entirely. Masculine virtue does permit a man occasional, crude artifacts of feeling: a boyish look down at his boots, a self-conscious kick in the dust, or an "aw, shucks, ma'am." It's emotional fluency, not emotion itself, that is off limits to the strong, silent man.

A Modern Cowboy

The story of a strong, silent man we'll call Charles is special, both because of its happy ending and because of the woman who made that ending possible. Charles met her under singularly unpromising circumstances. They were both residents of the Colonial Apartments on the north side of Nashville, Tennessee. Charles, twenty-five, had been living there for more than a year, waiting for his divorce to be finalized. The woman—we'll call her Karen—had just moved in after an unhappy love affair with a man in her home town. The last thing she wanted, she thought, was a romantic involvement. And the last place she expected to find it was the laundry room of the Colonial Apartments.

Charles was impatient because all the washing machines were full. So he stood holding his one-month accumulation of dirty laundry until the first machine clicked off. He lunged for it and began emptying the heavy clothes and piling them on the next machine. They were, of course, everything that he didn't want to find: bras, panties, slips, and several garments that he recognized but whose names and purposes were still unknown.

He wasn't half finished in his frantic subversion when Karen came down the basement stairs and saw him. "I didn't know what to think of him," she says, recounting with undisguised fondness their first, unlikely encounter. "When he looked up and saw me, he had a bra in each hand and he looked very guilty.

"By the time I'd snatched everything away and stuffed it in the dryer we were both laughing, and it seemed only natural to go off and have some coffee. He was *very* attractive to me," Karen remembers. "He's a big man, and he has a slow way of moving and a lovely slow smile. He told me he was a sound engineer at a country-and-western recording studio. He didn't say much, but when he asked me if I wanted to go dancing that Saturday, I was halfway in love.

"We saw a lot of each other after that, and right off the bat, I guess I did all the talking. Sometimes it seemed as though he had a lot of troubles stored up, but rather than try to find out what they were I just found myself wanting to entertain him. I think being with someone who is so laid back makes you anxious, so you keep up a nervous chatter. I thought he'd never ask me to marry him, and he didn't. I asked him." Exactly one year after their meeting in the basement laundry room, Charles and Karen married and moved to a small house in West Nashville.

But just as there is little room in John Wayne's cinema life for women, there was little room in Charles's life for Karen. In *Red River,* the woman Wayne supposedly loves pleads with him to take her along when he leaves the wagon train. Wayne refuses. "It's too much for a woman," he tells her. Later, when she is conveniently eliminated in an Indian raid, Wayne—his sexuality firmly established—is free to pursue his real goals in the world of men.

The same scenario—without the dire consequences—was played out in the lives of Charles and Karen. Like many women, Karen didn't begin to understand the implications of marrying a strong, silent man until it was too late. Only in retrospect did she see that Charles just "wasn't comfortable around women." So, with his marriage and home in order, Charles went back to his job, leaving Karen frustrated and alone.

His business affairs, however, were not so orderly. Soon after the wedding, Charles began to worry that his studio's plan to merge with another studio might squeeze him out of his job. As a strong, silent man, he couldn't share his anxieties directly; to do so would be to show unmanly weakness. So he tried to keep his home life and his work life separated by bottling up his fears. Instead of sharing his problems with Karen, he withdrew.

"He had two moods during that time," says Karen. "He

was either complaining: Why are we having chicken for dinner again? Why did I always leave the light on in the garage? Everything that went wrong was my fault. Or he was dead quiet. He would go out to his workroom and we wouldn't say a word to each other all weekend. Whenever he was one way, I thought the other way was easier to live with. We were like roommates, but roommates who didn't say good morning."

Karen realized that the problems in their relationship would never be solved until she confronted Charles directly. She had tried subtle hints. She had tried to get him to bring up problems by hinting around them. But Charles, like most strong, silent man, perceived her indirection as manipulation and resented it. He often retaliated by doggedly ignoring or resisting her invitations to "talk about it." Sometimes Karen felt that she was "dying" in the relationship, that there was no recourse except divorce.

For a while, she tried to cope with the loneliness. Then one morning as she was putting on her makeup for work, tears appeared in the mirror. Weeping openly, she walked into the kitchen where Charles looked up, startled, from his paper. "Charles," she said simply, "I need to be closer to you. We're so far apart, and I'm so lonely. I feel as though you've really left me. What can we do to be closer again?" Karen was lucky. Unlike a lot of men, Charles was able to respond.

"I want to be closer, too," he said.

The first battle every woman must fight in trying to help a strong, silent man express his feelings is the battle for his attention. If a man lives in two worlds, home and work, he may put a higher priority on the work world, and directing his attention to "intimate" problems at home can be especially difficult. A recent study by psychologist Ray Birdwhistle found that the average couple spends twenty-seven and a half minutes a week in conversation—a meager half hour. According to Dr. Marilyn Machlowitz, that includes "Would you pick up some milk?" "It's easy to see," says Machlowitz, "how adding a little talk could be unbelievably sexy."

Compounding the problem is the strong, silent man's general reluctance to talk about problems at all, or even acknowledge that there are any. Unless a woman can secure a man's attention, and ultimately his cooperation in the effort to establish emotional intimacy, that effort is not likely to succeed. A willingness to give must accompany any demand to receive.

It was overwhelming emotion that led Karen to confront Charles, and many women find that a calculated direct approach works far better then they ever imagined. Most men are, after all, accustomed to the politics of confrontation in their work. Yet many women in Karen's predicament are afraid to be direct, afraid to ask—in her words, "to know what's going on."

"I thought later," says Karen, "that there's an element of risk in all relationships. The friends of mine who have the best relationships are the ones who've learned that if rejection killed, we'd all be dead. They've learned that, so they're less afraid to confront the problems."

"Sometimes," says journalist Anne Gottlieb, "the [direct] approach is buried beneath the assumption—built up over the years—that the straightforward approach just won't work." Often, a woman can't express her needs because she isn't clear what they are. She knows that she's unhappy in the relationship, but she doesn't know why. Or she feels too proud to let a man know how much she needs his attention.

Instead of being direct, a woman may use a circumlocution, such as "Do you *have* to watch the game today?" Or, more often, she'll expect a man to give her the emotional feedback she needs without her having to ask for it, "on the grounds that a sensitive, loving man would simply know she needs more attention or more support or more conversation."

The fact is that a man may *not* be aware of what her needs are, and he may resent her indirect tactics as implied complaints. Most men actually prefer to hear needs and criticisms expressed directly, if at all. A drawn-out series of oblique hints will only make a man feel manipulated and cause his defenses to go up. For instance, if a woman isn't getting the physical affection she needs, says Dr. Daniel Casriel, "She must sit down and tell her partner that she has a strong need to be held and to be close. Men are traditionally supposed to take the lead," he observes, "but a woman has to teach a man what he doesn't know."

A man is also far more likely to respond to a request for intimacy if it is specific and presented in such a way that a specific solution is possible. "The morning of our confrontation I didn't just say 'open up' and leave it at that," says Karen. "It wasn't a showdown. It was a way of opening the door. Later, we went out to dinner and talked. I told Charles that in the morning I wanted him to say 'good morning.' I was tired of pretending the other person wasn't there. When he came home, I wanted him to put his arms around me. And if he didn't feel like it he could pretend I was Bo Derek. He got the idea. I wanted the *form* of openness, banking that the content would follow. And it did. Things really changed."

Karen was clear and specific about her emotional needs. By being up front about her expectations, a woman can guide the process of opening up and give a man objective criteria by which to evaluate his progress. If expectations are left ambiguous, success becomes increasingly elusive. A man may feel that he's being led on indefinitely, that the woman's expectations will never be fulfilled, and that further efforts are therefore bootless.

At each step of the way, Karen tried to make her needs explicit. When Charles, like many strong, silent men, came home from work tense, irritable, and inaccessible, she waded fearlessly into the problem. She described a typical conversation on such occasions:

"Charles, what's wrong?"

"Nothing."

"Charles, what happened today?"

"Nothing! Nothing happened today!"

"Gee, you sure look like something happened. You're pacing up and down. The phone rings and you jump." To break through the wall of silence and denials that surrounded him, Karen made her pleas direct, honest, and specific. "That's it, Charles," she would say. "I don't want to spend an evening with you if you're going to be like this. I really want you to tell me what happened today. Did you have another fight with a producer? Did one of your assistants mess up? Tell me what happened."

Because every man is different, every man will respond in his own way to a woman's efforts to open him up. Karen knew Charles well enough to know that he would probably respond positively if she confronted him. "But other men might have found that too demanding," she says. "I know women who give their husbands a little breathing space when they come home, maybe just a few minutes. Then they can talk about what's wrong. I just knew Charles well enough to know that if I'd left him alone, he would have sulked all evening."

Karen understood that Charles's cooperation was crucial to the success of her efforts. Walking into the kitchen and confronting him was one thing; enlisting his cooperation in a prolonged campaign to rejuvenate their relationship was something else. They were two people living under the same roof but carrying on different lives; neither their schedules nor their emotional needs intersected. Karen determined that she had to help them develop a shared life.

She started by leaving him a note whenever she left the house, telling him where she was going and when she'd be back. "We'd never done that before," she says. "I never knew he was going someplace until I heard the door close. We needed a sense of involvement in each other's lives, at a minimum. How can you do that if you don't know where the other person is? Charles saw the sense in that, because he started telling me whenever he went anywhere." Karen never asked him to leave notes; he learned from her example.

Setting an example of openness and intimacy requires,

above all, consistency. Charles finally was able to talk about his work problems, and Karen felt that she had opened the floodgates. She was in the living room talking with a friend when he came in with a complaint about his job. "I said something like 'Oh, come on now, Charles, it couldn't be all *that* bad,' " Karen remembers. " 'Stop complaining.' "

Charles walked out, partly puzzled and partly hurt, and then she realized what she had done. "During those years when he wasn't sharing anything with me," she says, "I just didn't foresee a time when I wouldn't want to hear him ask for help."

As Karen discovered, the process of overcoming a man's fear of intimacy is never simple. Years of playing the male role can't be undone with a magic word or two—an emotional open-sesame. The process is much more mechanical than magical. "There is no quick fix, no shortcut solution," Dr. Lewis Long told us. "Developing communication between a man and a woman takes time, patience, hard work, patience, pain, patience, love, patience."

Dr. Carlfred Broderick, a marital and family therapist at the University of Southern California, agrees: "The public is becoming more sophisticated about communication skills in marriages. No technique, however, can transcend a lack of individual commitment. . . . Unfortunately, we're better at teaching people how to meet their own needs than how to sacrifice, hang in there, and be patient. These are devalued virtues in American society. To make a [relationship] work," Dr. Broderick concludes, "you really need two things: *skill* and *will*."

"The trick," says Karen, "is to appreciate the little victories, like when he doesn't go straight to the TV set after dinner. A lot of women are waiting for a big victory that never comes. It's just a lot of little victories added up."

The Charmer

A Balance of Power

Most men maintain their masculine isolation by not showing the emotions they have: they feel but they can't (or won't) express their feelings. A few men, however, accomplish the same end by a different route. Instead of concealing emotions they have, they make a show of emotions they don't have. They master the forms of openness and intimacy while avoiding the substance. In the manly struggle not to make a genuine emotional connection, their tactics are diversionary rather than defensive. These are the charmers of the world.

The charmer, the lady's man, the Don Juan—almost every woman has a tale or two to tell about an interlude with a lady-killer. Those tales usually begin with words of love, well spoken, falling on eager ears. At first crush, the charmer is often a welcome relief to a woman—an oasis of compliments, consideration, and caring in a desert of masculine indifference. But the tales also have a common ending: as soon as the charmer's romantic campaign succeeds—in marriage, an affair, or just a night in bed—it abruptly ends. The great expectations of commitment and consideration, of sexual diversity and spiritual union, become just another set of unheeded demands. The oasis of masculine sympathy turns out to be a mirage.

The charmer is, basically, the same person Karen Horney characterizes as the "narcissist": a man with an "unquestioned belief in his [own] greatness and uniqueness. . . . His buoyancy and perennial youthfulness stem from this source. So does his often-fascinating charm. Yet clearly, his gifts notwithstanding, he stands on precarious ground. He may speak incessantly of his exploits or his wonderful qualities and needs endless confirmation of his estimate of himself in the form of admiration and devotion. His feeling of mastery lies in his conviction that there is nothing he cannot do and no one he cannot win.

"He is often charming indeed, particularly when new people come into his orbit. Regardless of their factual importance for him, he *must* impress them. He gives the impression to himself and others that he 'loves' [women]. And he can be generous, with a scintillating display of feeling, with flattery, with favors and help—in anticipation of admiration or in return for devotion received."

Because his surface charm doesn't rest on a foundation of genuine emotions, the charmer is often among the most closed of all closed men, and certainly among the most treacherous for women. Unlike the strong, silent man, whose inner life is active but hidden, the charmer has submerged his inner life in the "game"—the playact world in which he tries to win people is everything. His emotional world begins and ends with the repetitive quest for approval.

Just as the strong, silent man has been labeled "the cowboy" or "John Wayne" by psychologists, the charmer has been compared to James Bond and labeled "the playboy." Psychologists Balswick and Peek, who studied types of male behavior, concluded that while the playboy retains the cowboy's "emotional detachment and independence," his emotional problems are deeper.

"Bond and the playboy he caricatures," they write, "are in a sense 'dead' inside. They have no feelings toward women, while Wayne, although unwilling and perhaps unable to express them, does have such feelings." Although neither syndrome is desirable, it's psychologically less damaging to have feelings you can't express than to express feelings you don't have.

"The playboy's relationship with women," Balswick and Peek conclude, "represents the culmination of [Erich] Fromm's description of a marketing-oriented personality in which a person comes to see both himself and others as persons to be manipulated and exploited." The woman is reduced to an object, and ownership consists in conquest: "A successful 'love affair' is one in which the bed was shared, but the playboy emerges having avoided personal involvement or a shared relationship with the woman." The charmer, like Balswick and Peek's playboy, creates the romantic scene but remains removed from it.

Charmers come in many varieties. They range from the boy-who-never-grew-up, with his disarming smile and calculated naïveté, to what several women called the "lethal" kind—the kind who succeed at involving a woman totally. "It's the difference," one woman said, "between a high-school play and a Broadway show. A really great actor—and that's what a real Don Juan is—can make you forget he's acting. He makes *himself* forget. If he's good enough, most women don't want to know he's acting. They're eager to suspend their disbelief, their common sense, their better judgment. They'll suspend anything. He's that good."

The real Don Juan, or charmer, is confusing to a woman because he actually makes himself sensitive to a woman's needs. He notices what she likes and doesn't like, and he responds. And, of course, he usually is the good lover he's reputed to be.

A real charmer has a movie director's sense of mood and timing. He can choreograph seductions with startling ingenuity and imagination. Actress Linda Evans described such an occasion designed by her ex-husband John Derek; she came home to find John waiting for her "with champagne, and grapes that had been dipped in egg white and dusted with sugar, and a fur bed by the fireplace in a room full of candles." The mark of the real charmer is that the manipulativeness of such occasions is invisible. The appearance of sincerity, the impression that such moments are the untainted fruits of love, often makes the charmer irresistible.

Although the periodic approval of women is crucial to the charmer's self-esteem, his performances are not confined to romantic relationships. For him, all the world is a stage, and all the people in it an audience. The charmer is often popular in every forum where he performs: at parties, among friends at the office, with buddies at the gym or regulars at the bar. His charm is, by its nature, an impersonal, social charm—based on the shallow virtues and broad strokes of personality that carry well in a crowd. In groups, after all, there are no demands for personal sincerity. Ironically, that very popularity is often part of the charmer's attractiveness to women. They revel in the spotlight that seems to follow him around.

Despite the appearance of self-confidence and security, the charmer is, in fact, the most insecure of closed men. Far from being the self-confident manipulator he appears to be, according to Alfred Adler, "the Don Juan is a man who doubts his own manliness and is seeking constant additional evidence for it in his conquests."

Just as a Don Juan can be devastated when his sexual potency begins to falter, the charmer is exquisitely vulnerable to rejection. When his charm fails, when his power to win people wanes, he becomes—on his own terms, at least—impotent. Years of manipulative successes have drastically lowered his tolerance for failure. Even in a gender known for sensitive egos, the charmer's ego is particularly fragile.

The Allure of the Charmer

One man who fits the description of the charmer is Gordon. Born in the Midwest but educated in the East, Gordon settled in Washington, D.C., and rose quickly in the ranks of journalism. He can charm a story out of even the most reluctant source, and the same skills have served him well in his relationships with women.

Gordon has the dark good looks of a young Robert De Niro, a deep, expressive voice, an easy laugh, and a smooth social manner that makes even the most awkward encounter seem effortless. His envious friends assume, perhaps as a form of secret consolation, that Gordon's charm appeals only to a certain kind of woman—the young, unsuspecting ones who hang out near the corridors of power in hopes of being noticed by powerful men. In fact, Gordon's charm has always been more sophisticated, his art more subtle and convincing, and the women he wins more appealing than that. His secret? "It's simple," he tells friends who ask. "I understand women. I give them what they want."

Such was once the pattern of Gordon's romantic life: brief, windswept affairs—sometimes consecutive, sometimes simultaneous—but nothing that lasted. The first woman who succeeded in interrupting the rhythm of Gordon's romantic life was Vanessa.

There was something special about her from the start. She was attractive, certainly—with short blond "Lady Di" hair, and the perfect, matte complexion of a peach—but unlike most of Gordon's lady friends, she was not a beauty. While Gordon customarily found women at parties or in pursuit of a story, he didn't "find" Vanessa at all. Their meeting was arranged by a mutual friend.

At thirty, Vanessa was also at least five years older than most of the women Gordon had dated. She was an attorney in the litigation department of a small but highly regarded Washington law firm, and only a year or two away from partnership. She had a charming and disarming sense of humor, which attracted Gordon at their first encounter. Her wit was propelled by a sharp-edged intelligence.

No human foible passed by her unnoticed or unremarked—including Gordon's. "I was never completely under his spell, even from the start," she told us. "His reputation preceded him. I knew before our first date that he was a ladies' man and that he'd never been married. That always makes you a little suspicious."

Then why did she fall for him? "I was smitten. There were plenty of reasons." She opened her hand and began to count off on her fingers: "His looks, of course—I wasn't blind. His eyes. His body. That was enough to start. He was a great lover, too—the best lover I ever knew. When he touched me, it meant something. He really knew how to touch a woman. He was very alert to what I liked, what pleased me."

According to Vanessa, Gordon was as inventive in romance as he was in lovemaking. "He was a master of the unexpected. He loved surprises and games and could be very playful. One night I arrived at his apartment and he said, 'Let's go up on the roof. I want to show you something.' And there it was, a beautiful picnic dinner, all laid out like in an Italian movie. I loved it."

Gordon also liked to take Vanessa on spontaneous mini-vacations: a night here, a weekend there, unplanned trips to romantic spots. "Everything he did was directed at keeping the relationship fresh, like new. He was so imaginative, always keeping you guessing about what he would do next. He was always calling with something new to say or some new plans. Most men hate to use the telephone, but not Gordon."

But it wasn't just the surface things, Vanessa was quick to add—good as they were. "He was really interested in *me*. He cared how I felt. He asked me what *I* wanted to do, where *I* wanted to eat. He listened to me—he sat for hours and asked me questions. I'd never had a man do that before. Maybe it was his training as a reporter, but you can bet that a lawyer wouldn't sit and listen to anyone talk for hours on end, especially a woman."

For Vanessa, Gordon's primary romantic asset was his ability to make her feel special. "When we were together, it didn't matter whether it was just the two of us in a quiet restaurant or we were caught in a crowd, he made me feel like I was the only person in the room—the only person in the *world*. He has this wonderful ability to focus all his attention and charm on one person, and it makes you feel beautiful and special regardless of what the mirror says."

She remembered Gordon's way of leaning toward her, his head in his hand, seemingly lost in her thoughts. "He made you think he was screening out all distractions. He didn't want to see anything else in the world. He didn't care about anybody else. It was all for you. I was so used to hardness and inattention from men, this was like water in the desert. It was as if you took a plant from hard, dry ground and transplanted it in a warm, sunny greenhouse in rich black soil and gave it plenty of water. I thrived on the attention."

But just when Vanessa began to let down her guard and consider Gordon as a serious lover and possible mate, his behavior changed.

"After a marvelous weekend on Cape Cod, I called him and he sounded distant," she told us. "He said he'd be tied up for the next week on a special assignment. It was a real bitch and he'd call when he could. It was something of a shock, but it didn't take me long to realize what was happening. I had been warned and I was seeing it firsthand. After two weeks went by I made a decision: I would not join the ranks of women around town he'd left—I was going to leave him first. I sent him a note saying it had been lovely but I realized he really wasn't the kind of man I was looking for.

"Months passed. I was miserable, but wild horses couldn't have made me call. I heard he was seeing someone else. Then, of course, as I think I knew he would, he called and said he'd like to see me again. I refused—and the more I refused, the more attention he paid. It was like a law of physics. But I truly wasn't interested in him or his manipulations anymore.

"Then he did something that was so wonderfully calculated and delightful that I cracked. I was expecting a *New York Times* reporter to arrive for an interview on women lawyers. The reporter arrived and it was Gordon. He played the role absolutely straight until we both burst out laughing. To clinch it, after he left I discovered that when I was out of the room he had put a framed photograph of himself on my mantel. The inscription read, 'I love Vanessa.' It was just so mad and marvelous and absolutely diabolical.

"We began seeing each other again, but it was different this time. I began to turn down his invitations to fancy restaurants and diplomatic receptions. The second time around the track, I really began to rebel at his smoothness, his familiar way of relating to women. I kept a little more of myself in reserve. I wasn't so quick to be carried away on charm alone."

That hint of aloofness was what kept Gordon interested. Gordon's past had been little more than a series of brief affairs, each lasting only as long as a woman held out against his seductive powers. Like most charmers, Gordon couldn't resist a challenge. Women who surrendered too soon or too easily held no interest for him. He liked seducing women, and without the challenge of resistance, seduction was a joyless exercise. By stepping back to just beyond his grasp, Vanessa suddenly became very interesting.

"I began to realize that if I wanted a real relationship with Gordon, I needed to maintain a balance of power. That idea excited me. I guess I'm a very independent person and I found the notion of another *very* independent person challenging. We've sort of recognized ourselves in each other—and for three years now I've been very happy with Gordon. A charmer will always be a charmer. He just can't help himself. But there are these wonderful open spaces in between when he isn't trying to entertain or impress anyone, when he's just himself. At times like that, he's the best—*we're* the best."

The Loner

"Let Him Freeze"

When sex therapist Dr. Helen Singer Kaplan was asked "what's the best way to make a marriage work?" she answered unequivocally: "Choose the right partner! With the wrong partner, no matter how hard you work, the marriage is not likely to succeed. . . . Too many people marry without understanding their own needs and their partner's needs."

Some women, unfortunately, forget to ask themselves the crucial first question: *Can* he open up? Is he "a butterfly waiting in his chrysalis" for a woman to set him free, or is he so captive to childhood conditioning and social pressures that he is unlikely ever to open up, no matter how much effort is made or how much help is offered? Women who lament failed relationships—both past and current—with closed men sometimes don't stop to consider that those relationships may have been ill-fated from the inception. Instead, they blame the man ("He didn't know how good he had it"), they blame men as a gender ("They're all zombies"), or, most often, they blame themselves ("If only I'd tried harder").

Sometimes there really is no one to blame. The fault lies not in the man's perversity, or his gender's hostility, or the woman's inadequacy. The fault, unfortunately, lies in the fact that some men are fundamentally closed off to emotional intimacy. Whatever efforts a woman may make, however hard she may pry at the cover or bang at the gates, these men are almost predestined to live alone. Most of them might change only with years of professional therapy, which, of all men, they have the least motivation or ability to undertake.

Unlike most men, who fear intimacy but want desperately to build an emotional bridge to another person and end their isolation, the loner seems relatively resigned to being marooned on the island of his indifference. He is emotionally self-sufficient, as much as anyone can be. He may have relationships, but they are devoid of commitment. "Some men are like long-distance runners," one woman told us. "They stop to rest for a minute and they call that a relationship. But the only place they feel at home is on the road."

Some women are drawn to the loner, attracted by his aloofness from the world, the allure of the unknown, and what they mistakenly see as the needfulness of his isolation. "He appealed to the mother in me," said one woman, who discovered too late that her husband was "an emotional gypsy" and divorced him after only a few years of marriage. "I thought, 'Oh, this poor lonely man, he needs someone to love him.' But he didn't—deep down he really *didn't* need someone. His parents had never really given him any love, so he didn't know what a loving relationship was. It still makes me sad when I think of it—there's still part of me that wants to give him the love he never had—but I'm glad I realized it would never work, before it ruined both our lives."

The attractiveness of the loner is very much like the attractiveness of the strong, silent man. By being aloof and unflappable, he creates the illusion of strength. His inaccessibility is taken for substance and reliability. Add to these attractions the romantic challenge of the "unobtainable" man, and the allure of the loner—for some women, at least—is complete. That's why it's so important for susceptible women to know how to detect a loner, how to tell if a man is truly beyond emotional reach, and when to accept as a fact that he truly is unobtainable.

In particular, a woman must develop the ability to distinguish between a loner—a man who has serious psychological difficulties that probably require long-term professional care —and a charmer or a workaholic—someone who probably can be helped in the context of a relationship, without outside assistance.

Is He a Loner?

The loner is detached in all of his social contacts, careful at all times to keep his emotional distance from others. A woman in a long-term relationship should always be suspicious of a man who won't make an emotional commitment to her, but she should be especially wary of a man who can't make any kind of emotional commitment, even to a parent or a friend. The loner is, according to Karen Horney, someone who "can enjoy distant or transitory relationships, but [who feels] he should not become emotionally involved. He should not become so attached to a person as to need [her] company, [her] help, or sexual relations with [her] . . . he does not expect much, either good or bad—if anything— from others."

A woman in Minnesota, who has been married to her second husband for twenty years, spoke to us about her first husband, a true loner. "I should have seen the signs," she said. "He wasn't affectionate, he was always distracted, but I tended to blame myself. I hadn't been with many men, so when we were married I didn't have much to compare him to. I thought he didn't love me because I was unlovable. I didn't stop to ask myself why he didn't have any friends, why we never invited his colleagues to the house for dinner. Then one day his sister and her husband came to visit, and he could barely keep a conversation going. It all clicked. He didn't love me not because I was unlovable but because he couldn't love anyone."

Because the true loner has so much trouble with emotional intimacy, a woman might naturally assume that he is not capable of sexual intimacy either. In fact, few loners are so badly handicapped that they avoid sex altogether, but most avoid combining emotional intimacy and physical intimacy in the same act. The way a loner maintains emotional distance from a sexual partner varies. "He may exclude sex as being too intimate for a permanent relationship," according to Horney, "and instead satisfy his sexual needs with a stranger [or] he may more or less restrict a relationship to merely sexual contacts and not share other experience with the partner."

There are some loners who are so withdrawn that they avoid relationships altogether: "Avoiding relationships," Dr. Garfield told us, "can be a sign of a withdrawn, schizoid type of personality. A man who can't love himself is a man to worry about, a man who won't venture out into the world of relationships because it is too threatening. He won't risk exposing himself or risk learning about himself. These are some of the signposts indicating that a person really needs to look at himself, that he really needs some professional counseling and help."

A loner is usually indifferent to the reactions of people around him. Of course, many closed men make a pretense of not caring what others think, because indifference is a part of the masculine role they play. The true loner, however, has learned not to care, not to be hurt by what others think. Sometimes a loner may share his problems but react to the problems of others with thinly veiled disinterest. Or he may listen endlessly to others' problems but never reveal his own. Without the reciprocity necessary for intimacy, his relationships remain shallow, one-sided, and impersonal.

Dr. Joseph Luft, a professor of psychology at San Francisco State University and author of *Of Human Interaction*, has devised questions to help people determine when a relationship is sufficiently "reciprocal" for genuine intimacy to develop:

• Is there an ongoing relationship that provides a context for emotional expressiveness, or do those moments of openness exist in a vacuum?

• When a man expresses his feelings, is he aware of how others are reacting?

• Is he concerned that his feelings have meaning in the other person's life, or is he just "letting off steam" to relieve inner pressure?

Living with a Loner

The loner's inability to share emotional needs with others makes a long-term relationship unlikely, but not impossible. On the one hand, there are some women who, for their own psychological reasons, want a relationship in which they can feel protected by considerable emotional separation. Their need for independence is so strong that they prefer a man who will give them the ample emotional space they require. Other women have so much need to give emotional reassurance, and so little need to receive it, that they can survive remarkably well on the regimen of sustained unilateral devotion that life with a loner often becomes.

"Like most girls, I was once madly in love with a musician," Marlo, a thirty-five-year-old woman who works as a congressional aide in Washington, told us. "Geoff was a marvelous cellist, totally devoted to music. Of course, he had practically no time for me." Marlo followed Geoff faithfully to concerts, standing in the back "with glassy eyes," she recalled. "I wanted to think the music was just for me." For six months, she carried his music, sat and watched while he practiced, and generally "arranged my life around him."

During all that time, while Marlo was working on Capitol Hill, Geoff never joined her in a political discussion or asked about her life beyond his practice room or the concert halls. "I used to make excuses for him," Marlo said. "His music was everything to him, so it was everything to me—for a while. Then I realized he was just plain selfish. My aunt told me, 'Never get involved with an artist. They're married to their work.' I was too love-struck to listen at the time. But she was right. Maybe not all musicians, but it was true of Geoff. When I realized that, the relationship was over."

Not long after Marlo broke off their relationship, Geoff married a young woman who was a cello student of his. Unlike Marlo, she was willing to get in line behind music in Geoff's life, to become a permanent groupie. "She carted him around from one concert to another, ran his errands, rosined his bow," Marlo told us. "She was willing to play second fiddle for the rest of her life. That may be what she wanted, but it wasn't for me."

Sometimes, even women who need true intimacy go through their entire lives with men who are not capable of providing it. Because they feel too much empathy for the men they love, because they don't want to give up the challenge of finding intimacy with them, or simply because they don't know what else to do, they spend their lives fighting battles they can't win. But for others, the futility of that fight is a wisdom that comes early in life. A woman we'll call Sarah was one of the luckier ones: David was the first and last true loner of her romantic life.

She met him at Princeton, where they both studied physics and both belonged to an eating club called Stevenson

Hall. Eating clubs, like fraternities, tend to develop personalities over time, and Stevenson was the "nerd" club—although they used the word *wonk* then. It was not a typical Princeton club, Sarah noted. There were no croquet wickets on the lawn outside, no white pants in the spring (who even noticed the seasons changing?), and no straw hats. At Stevenson, calculators outnumbered Lacoste shirts, and the nightly episode of "Star Trek" drew a far bigger crowd than the big game on Saturday. In short, Stevenson Hall was the logical meeting place for Princeton's loners.

Basically, what Sarah remembered about David could be told in a paragraph. He was a physics student and, according to the low-voltage gossip circuit at Stevenson, the most brilliant science type to wander aimlessly through the labs of Princeton since Albert Einstein. When David wasn't working—and perhaps even when he was—he shambled about with untied shoes and a blank look in his eyes. There were some at Stevenson who playacted the spaced-out genius. They were infatuated with the image of unspoiled intellect and unselfconscious nonconformity. But David was no playactor. His mind *was* elsewhere. He was a loner through and through—already and irretrievably married to his own thoughts.

The only woman who found her way to the center of David's emotional world was Sarah. She told us how she had left home in Montclair, New Jersey, after her junior year in high school; parental interference was cramping her style. Something of a loner herself, she moved into her own apartment and worked as a night "copy-boy" for a New York newspaper, commuting to high school in Montclair. At Princeton, Sarah joined Stevenson partly because the food was good and cheap, but mostly because it was the most nonsocial club on Prospect Avenue. No one bothered to make small talk at the table or socialize afterward, so a woman with lots to do (which Sarah was) could get in and out quickly.

Although Sarah was too busy to notice much at Stevenson, she did notice David. She knew his reputation, and she was fascinated both by the remote power of his intellect and by the challenge of his inaccessibility. David had been watching her too from behind the gauze of indifference and self-absorption that separated most of the students at Stevenson. Their first conversation over lunch was no more than four or five sentences, but by Stevenson standards it was a Platonic dialogue. It emboldened her to speak to him again the next time she whirled in for a meal.

Soon, Sarah began to come more regularly to Stevenson, hand in hand with David, and to stay longer. They had begun to date. She took him to his first movie since childhood. They went to New York City for a weekend. They spent hours together in his laboratory.

Then, suddenly, three months later, David and Sarah stopped coming in together. "I tried to bring him out," she explained to us, "but I discovered there wasn't that much to bring out.

"I have a very strong reaction to men I'm involved with," she said, "when they try to shut me out of what's going on inside them. David was like that, and nothing I did seemed to help. There are just so many times you can rally your troops for another assault."

Sarah told us she came from a family of women—three sisters and a mother—who were very closed. When she was growing up, she never accepted the stereotype that women were open and men were closed. She knew only that everyone in her family was closed. "My mother would yell, 'I'm *not* angry!' And she never saw the incredible schizophrenia behind that. My family never believed in talking about feelings. Except anger, of course. Instead, they shoved everything under the rug. I used to tell people, 'There's an elephant in our living room, but it's under the rug. It's creating an enormous lump under the rug in front of the sofa, even though our family swears the floor is flat.'

"I guess I was unconsciously attracted to David because he was like someone in my family. But I soon found out that he was really closed. And I found out that when people don't reveal vulnerability, I guess I just can't relate to them as human beings. It's one thing to work with them. I can deal with them that way. But on a personal level, it's no fun. There's no sharing of experience.

"As far as I'm concerned, there are some men who are so closed that there's not much you or anybody can do about it, at least not in one lifetime. I try not to have anything to do with a man like that in the first place. Once burned, twice cautious. I'm just glad I found out so early."

Sarah's advice is useful to most women confronted with the possibility of a relationship with a loner: no man is beyond emotional reach, but a few men are so emotionally distant that a woman should think twice before making the effort to reach them. "I agree with that old Lena Horne line," says Sarah, " 'if your man's too cold, let him freeze.' "

The Workaholic

Putting the Relationship on the Line

For millions of men (and women) work is the beginning and end of passion. Many women can tick off on their fingers the symptoms of workaholism: up at dawn; a preoccupied breakfast; days out of reach; message after message left with secretaries; a phone call around five: "I won't be home for dinner"; the door opening at nine, ten, eleven, or later; phone calls in the night and on that rare Sunday at home; unexpected cancellations and interrupted vacations; and always, even in bed, that intractable preoccupation with work.

Karen Horney's description of the "perfectionist" fits many extreme workaholics: "Perfectionists, in a streamlined way, are bent on self-glorification, on ambitious pursuits . . . with the mastery of life through intelligence and will power as the means to actualize their idealized self."

In this headlong pursuit of the "idealized self," a man's "real self" is often lost—and so is the possibility of intimacy. The workaholic, says Lotte Bailyn of M.I.T., is the "victim of a newly recognized social disease presumably responsible for the disintegration of the family, [and] for severe distortion of full personal development."

Intimacy requires time, yet most workaholics operate with a budget deficit of time. "The greatest tragedy in life," a seemingly easygoing but privately work-obsessed lawyer, told us, "is that there are only twenty-four hours in a day." But even as he complains about the surfeit of work and the scarcity of time, the workaholic glories in his "busyness." He becomes so entangled in it that people become merely additional entries on his agenda, their urgency and his attention dependent on his work schedule, not apart from it.

When a wife or lover asks him about work, the question comes like a short circuit: details don't ask about other details. Women tend to become not colleagues but employees, requiring direction and paternal advice, not respect and intimacy. "The most successful men, workaholics," says Dr. Sol Landau, head of the Mid-Life Services Foundation in Dade County, Florida, "[are] unconnected to their personal lives." Dr. Mortimer R. Feinberg, a New York psychologist, calls workaholics "corporate bigamists," because they often seem more interested in their companies than in their wives.

The extreme workaholic often leads a life of professional success and personal unhappiness. An officer of a Fortune 500 company in New York tells of the relationship between her boss, the chairman and CEO, and his wife of more than thirty years. "He was always so proud that he'd been able to give her everything she could ever hope for—a beautiful home in Greenwich, a magnificent wardrobe, a tennis court and swimming pool, servants, a car and driver, the works.

"But she was miserable. He used to go to the office at five thirty in the morning, six or seven days a week, and never came home before ten, if he didn't just spend the night in the company apartment in Manhattan. He never saw how unhappy she was—unhappy, bored, and lonely." Like many workaholics, he gave his wife everything she could have hoped for, except the one thing she really wanted: him.

What can make a workaholic open up? Under what circumstances will he stop his almost frantic race against himself long enough to look around and notice those near him? What can make him understand both the needs of those who love him and his own need for love?

In a way, the workaholic is often too successful for his own good. With such an impressive show of outward accomplishment, he often succeeds in suppressing feelings of anxiety, melancholy, and boredom. As Horney says, he "eliminates all traces of self-doubt." Because he hides so well from his own feelings, the typical workaholic faces his problems only if something forces him to face them.

The most common trigger for this kind of life change is a crisis—some major disruption in the pounding rhythm of the workaholic's routine that forces him to reexamine his life, himself, his role, and his relationships. "Nothing short of a major crisis," says Dr. Marilyn Machlowitz in *Workaholics,* "spurs them to think about their workaholism."

Although the crisis may take a number of forms—death of a loved one, career reversal, major illness—the most common form is the collapse, or potential collapse, of a relationship. When a woman's magazine recently surveyed men who had learned to open up and asked them what events or persons triggered the radical changes they made in learning to express their feelings, the most common answer was "experiencing a major crisis in love and/or work." Hard though it may sound, many women have found that the only way to make an extreme workaholic open up is to let him know that the relationship is on the line.

An American Success Story

That was how one closed man finally opened up. We'll call him Dan. Until about four years ago, Dan's friends thought he was the perfect American success story. Born with exceptional athletic ability, Dan responded to the coaxing of his father, a high-school baseball coach who had decided in the maternity-ward waiting room that his son would be a professional baseball player.

For a while Dan succeeded brilliantly in this vicarious life, eventually captaining his college team while doing well enough to be accepted at a major law school. More than anything, Dan wanted to be successful. Whatever "real self" there was in him, he was eager to cash it in for a guarantee of unlimited upward mobility.

The energy of the workaholic is as protean as sexual libido; the forms it takes are usually accidental, not inevitable. The typical workaholic can be obsessed with any activity toward which circumstances direct him, from corporate mergers to pasta making. When Dan graduated from college and was deprived of athletics as an outlet for his furious energies, he redirected those energies, without skipping a beat, into the law.

In fact, his drive was redoubled. If he had been determined before, now he was positively obsessed. He became editor of the school law review, landed a plum of a clerking job with a federal district judge in San Francisco, and then a position with a small but highly respected corporate law firm in Los Angeles. He billed more hours his first year (an average of seventy-five per week) than any of his fellow workaholics. When he was made a partner in the firm—in record time—he "celebrated" by having a bathroom and shower constructed in his office to accommodate his frequent overnight work binges.

Most of Dan's partners viewed his blind devotion to his work with considerable favor, but his wife, whom we'll call Susan, looked on it with mixed feelings. Like many women married to successful men, she enjoyed his success vicariously, but resented having so little time with him. In the first few years after their marriage, she had hoped that things would change, that Dan would let down, relax, and take the time to give her the attention she needed and the affection he professed to feel. She had wanted to have a child, but had trouble conceiving. Each of Dan's victories brought only new ambitions, new battles, new competition, and left her feeling increasingly alone.

Unwillingly, Susan began to wonder if she and Dan would ever feel as close as they had that day, seemingly long ago, when he had worked so hard, and with such success, to win her love. "Sure, it *looked* like the perfect marriage," says Susan now. "What woman could have asked for more than Dan: handsome, ambitious, smart. How often do you say 'no thank you' to a man like that?"

But it was easy for Susan to say "no thank you" to his long days, and sometimes nights, away from her. "I had a job too, but that didn't mean I had no time for him," she says. "After each big case, I thought it would get better." But it didn't. It got worse. And Susan began to question all the assumptions on which their relationship was based. Did Dan love her? Did she love him? Did they have a life together?

When she would broach the subject of their growing separation, Dan didn't seem to care. His attitude was typical: it was just another one of her "little tantrums," and it would pass. In a way, it would. Except that the hurt kept building up, until Susan knew that something would have to give. "Either I had to budge him or I had to leave. I just couldn't take it any longer."

It was only at this point, when Susan determined that she couldn't communicate her pain, that she decided to leave. There was nothing else left to do. "If I hadn't been serious about leaving for good," she says, "I think he would have seen it as just another gesture, another of my 'little tantrums.' "

When Susan told Dan she was leaving, packed an overnight bag, and walked out of the house, Dan was devastated. Like most workaholics confronted with a major crisis, he felt failure for the first time in his life. He suffered the fate Karen

Horney says all "perfectionists" suffer when tragedy strikes: "[When] any misfortune befalls him, such as the loss of a child, an accident, the infidelity of his wife, the loss of a job, [it] may bring this seemingly well-balanced person to the verge of collapse. He not only resents ill fortune as unfair but, over and beyond this, is shaken by it to the foundations of his psychic existence. It invalidates his whole accounting system and conjures up the ghastly prospect of helplessness."

In typical workaholic fashion, Dan didn't realize how much he depended on Susan. Behind his seeming indifference and real inattention, he needed her constant and unquestioning support to maintain the illusion of perfection and control. By leaving him, she forced him to face the truths that had always been conveniently obscured by his success: that he needed her as much as, if not more than, she needed him; that he could not live successfully without her; that her departure was at least partly the product of his imperfections. This last admission, the admission of imperfection, of failure, is the hardest for the workaholic to make. He had always thought their relationship was an accomplished fact. Now he realized that he had to "accomplish" that relationship anew every day.

When she left Dan, Susan went to her sister's and cried for a day. The next morning, she decided: "No more tears." "My sister thought I should walk away and not look back," she recalls. "I was seduced by that attitude at first. I had made my stand, I'd taken decisive action, and I was pretty proud of myself. I developed a kind of emotional swagger—you know, 'I am invincible,' that sort of nonsense. Nobody's invincible. I played Wonder Woman for a few weeks before I realized how unhappy I was."

Just as she was beginning to have second thoughts, a letter arrived from Dan. He admitted his faults in abject terms and pleaded with her to return. "It was not at all like Dan," she says, "to accept all the blame himself. I knew it must have been agony for him to write."

Whether or not a man responds to a crisis by opening up depends primarily on the reactions of people around him to his new vulnerability. When Dan sent Susan the letter, he was saying, for the first time in their relationship, "I need you. I'm not strong enough to live without you." For Dan, the admission of weakness was a breakthrough. He was reaching out the only way he knew how, and perhaps, in a way, he knew Susan would respond.

Dan's letter sent Susan into a "tailspin" of doubt and anxiety but also gave her cause for hope. "What could I say to that?" she asks rhetorically. "He was asking for help, and for Dan, that must have been excruciating." From that moment, Susan knew she would respond, and she knew they would get back together. It was just a question of how.

Accept His Need for Work

Recognizing a workaholic's addiction for what it is, one New York psychologist told us, is an important step toward coping with it. Dan came away from his crisis with a renewed awareness of Susan's needs, but Susan also came away from it with a renewed awareness of Dan's needs: his need to work hard, his need to achieve. Susan came to realize that deep inside Dan there was still a little boy fighting to please the world with home runs and teachers' praise. She also realized that his desire for achievement was part of what had initially attracted her to him, and that it would always be an essential aspect of his personality.

Many women are so deeply upset by the problems they face in breaking through a man's devotion to work, in dealing with the loneliness, the time apart, the sense of "second fiddle," that they overlook the importance of his workaholism both to his personality and to his attractiveness. A woman is often drawn to a workaholic man precisely because he *is* a workaholic. Many women find it helpful simply to imagine what the relationship would be like if the man were not a workaholic. What if he were just a plain nine-to-fiver?

"I saw Rodney for about eight months," says Jennifer, a dietitian in New Canaan, Connecticut, "before I got too jealous of his job. At night I wanted to go out to dinner, to the movies. All he wanted to do was put in overtime at his computer lab." So Jennifer started seeing someone else, who at first seemed perfect. He was always ready for dinner or a movie. He had a job with a hotel chain which he hated and never talked about. Jennifer soon discovered why. "He didn't just hate his job," she says, "he hated everything. Everything bored him, so he was boring. It wasn't long before I missed Rod's intensity. Maybe he doesn't want to go to the movies, but at least he loves what he does."

Try to Become a Part of His Work

If a man is totally taken up in his working world, the best way to enter his world is through his work. The man and woman who work together are particularly lucky. The most successful relationships are often built on the foundations of a joint career. Working together provides an inexhaustible source of nonemotional problems to analyze, issues to discuss, and possibilities to explore.

For couples who must work apart, the best solution is to become as involved in each other's careers as possible. "It's well worth the effort," says one expert, "to see that you and any other family members are exposed to the workaholic's work world." That means visiting the workaholic's workplace and getting to know his colleagues. It also means joining him on business trips from time to time. "Sometimes," the expert adds, "your own work schedule or personal preferences preclude tagging along on the workaholic's business trip. But once in a while is fine, and even a child can be snatched out of school for an occasional trip."

Bernice, a fortyish woman in Tulsa, Oklahoma, related to us her experience in the working world of her workaholic husband, Tom, the owner of a pipe company in Tulsa. "Tom eats, sleeps, and breathes his business," says Bernice. "He knows more than any man alive about pipes." When Bernice married Tom twenty years ago, she had a passion for the fine arts, especially serious films.

"Well, I didn't give a fig about pipes, so it seemed boring to me, even though I was happy Tom was so successful at it. Tom felt the same way about films. His idea of a movie was watching Burt Reynolds on TV. So for a few years we were at a standoff and didn't see much of each other." Finally, in desperation for something to do, Bernice got a volunteer job managing a hospital thrift shop. Through her job, she began to learn the rudiments of business. Slowly, she began to develop a genuine, if not voracious, interest in Tom's work.

"We talked mostly about business for a while, but then the conversation began to open out into all sorts of things we'd never talked about before." For Bernice, learning to talk about business was like building a bridge between two islands. Once it was there, other forms of "commerce" became possible.

Teach the Workaholic to "Play"

A workaholic can sometimes be diverted from his obsession by extracurricular activity, or play. Although play comes hard to him, once engaged he's likely to bring to it the same intensity that he brings to work. "My husband is every bit as fanatical about his golf as he is about his work," says a woman married to a workaholic lawyer in New York. "He breaks clubs, yells at balls, tries to bribe the scorekeeper, and drives the caddies crazy. It's just business as usual for him."

One way to approach the workaholic is to start with forms of play that can be viewed as projects, so that he has a sense of achievement while he's enjoying himself. One woman living with such a man gave him a copy of *Beard on Bread* and a supply of yeast and special flours for his birthday. They now bake bread together every Saturday morning. The wife of another workaholic, who learned that her husband had enjoyed camping as a boy, organized trips to the best camping sites on the eastern seaboard. They now spend a great deal of time together under his L. L. Bean tent planning ever more elaborate expeditions.

Another woman married to an intensely work-committed man made herself one of his projects. Early in their relationship, she established that her needs and plans were as important as his, even though he was already a successful Broadway producer. To the surprise of her friends, his calls from the Coast were often not about what star had just signed to play the lead in a show he was producing, but about her drawing classes at the museum. She went on to become a professional designer and took her turn calling him from the Coast, but the pattern she set early in their relationship meant that she had his attention whether or not her career matched his. Although his work life is still going twenty-four hours a day, she is one of his projects that's never finished —and he is one of hers.

Make an Independent Life

To break the cycle of expectation and disappointment, a wife often finds that she has to have a life independent of her husband, a life so fulfilling that she no longer resents being left alone during the hours he spends—and will always spend—at work.

"Anticipate spending a lot of time on your own," says one psychologist. "This may mean more time to 'do your own thing,' more time for your own work, or more time to see the friends your workaholic mate can't stand. Interests and independence are critical qualities for anyone who aspires to live with a workaholic." If both the man and woman have careers, they can share their professions.

At the very least, the woman married to a workaholic needs her own obsessions. Workaholics will never become easygoing, pipe-and-slippers men, nor would their wives or lovers be satisfied if they did. But women can help men to avoid what one woman called "the Bermuda Triangle" of workaholism, the total obsessive oblivion into which a person sinks out of intimacy's reach.

Therapy

When Outside Help Is Needed

SOME COUPLES DEVELOP a pattern of distrust so strong that it's very difficult to break. Instead of stating their feelings and then responding to each other, they state their demands and then condemn each other. Each new effort at resolving their problems falls quickly into the same rut; each new conversation becomes a replay of the conversation before. In such cases, the best solution may be to meet with an impartial third party, someone who can help a couple recognize their hurtful patterns of communication—or *mis*communication— in order to break out of them.

Dr. Lewis Long was one of many experts who recommended outside, though not necessarily professional, help. "The trouble with many relationships," he told us, "is that they try to build from too small a base—a twosome. Most of us need help and stimulation and guidance from the outside. It doesn't matter if that help comes from a family member, a therapist, or a minister, as long as it comes from the outside."

"People say things to a therapist," a man named Jordan told us, "even in the presence of the other, that they won't say to each other. The therapist would say things that Marsha had always said, but when she said them I didn't believe her. When *he* said them, they were easier to accept because they were the opinions of a neutral third party. The therapist is a referee, someone who can say, 'This is how it is.' "

A History of Holding Back

For Robert and Lynn, one couple we spoke to who sought outside assistance, the road to confidence, self-worth, and openness was filled with surprises. For as long as anyone could remember, there had always been something elusive about Robert, some part of him that held back. His living space, like his life, was always excruciatingly neat. On his dresser, a comb, razor, aftershave, and talc looked as if they'd been arranged on a piece of graph paper.

But underneath, Robert's life was less than tidy. His father, the son of Polish immigrants, was a cop in the working-class Hampden section of Baltimore. Robert's mother, like his father, did not graduate from high school. She worked in a big commercial bakery, mixing the dough which became the rolls that Lynn, an attorney, ate when she took clients to Baltimore's best restaurants.

Robert was embarrassed by his parents—by their lower-class, immigrant background, their lack of education, their living conditions, their jobs. He always deflected inquiries about his home and family. He was too proper to lie, but too embarrassed to discuss them. When pressed, he would blurt out his father's profession as if it were an admission of guilt.

Robert, like most people, wanted to surround himself with the things he didn't have as a child. "It is the feeling of inferiority, inadequacy, insecurity, which determines the goal of an individual's existence," writes Alfred Adler in *Understanding Human Nature*. "The tendency to push into the limelight, to compel the attention of parents, makes itself felt in the first days of life."

As soon as he could, Robert sought friends among the

wealthy and/or purebred. When he arrived at Amherst College, he joined the right clubs, was seen in the right places with the right people. He reveled in the companionship of sophisticated people whose easy familiarity with art and music and the finer things in life reflected his idealized self. He learned to speak French and to wax eloquent over a good bottle of wine. He longed to travel and talk casually about exotic places.

When he brought his search to medical school at Johns Hopkins, he found the girl of his fantasies, Lynn, the daughter of a prominent San Francisco attorney, and scion of an old Nob Hill family. She took him to the family's mansion overlooking the Bay, where Robert sat amid the fine porcelain and silver talking about literature with her mother and thinking how far he was from his parents and their Baltimore row house.

Once he married Lynn, Robert seemed to have it all: the status and "class" he longed for, a promising career, a caring wife. But, inside, he saw himself still as the son of a Polack cop. His successes only intensified his feelings of inadequacy. He explained them to himself by saying: "I don't deserve it."

Even before the wedding, Lynn knew that life with Robert would not be easy. "I saw how he dealt with people," Lynn admitted to us. "I knew he could be pompous and condescending, especially when we were in company. But he wasn't like that when we were alone." At first Lynn thought that his arrogance was a product of youthful insecurity, and as he got older and more successful, he would have less to prove to the world and his behavior would change. In fact, exactly the reverse happened. With age, Robert only grew more insecure, acting more difficult and overbearing on the outside, and feeling more fearful and needful on the inside.

Even when Lynn began to recognize the problem, there was little she could do about it. The last thing Robert could do was admit his own insecurity. The whole facade would come tumbling down. Even if he could have admitted it to someone, he could never have admitted it to Lynn. "I was the last person he could talk to," she said. "But I was the only person close to him—so he ended up not talking to anybody." Marooned on the island of their marriage, Robert was unable to communicate with his only companion.

By the time he entered his first year of residency, heavy demands on his time tended to conceal the problem. And Lynn had a new concern of her own: she was pregnant. He worked long hours, and she had plenty of female friends to carry the days. By the time he was appointed to a prestigious position at Johns Hopkins, she was in her third pregnancy and they were virtual strangers.

Like many women married to closed men, Lynn called a temporary truce and abandoned—for the time being, she told herself—her quest for genuine intimacy with Robert. Her emotional needs were largely satisfied by her three children.

But after the last of them entered first grade, Lynn began to think again about her relationship with Robert and how unsatisfying it had become. The same stale problems still hung in the air between them, but now she felt guilty for having ignored them, for having turned away from Robert. She also realized that if she did nothing to put their emotional lives back in order, she would be condemned to years of loneliness, biding her time until the kids were old enough not to be traumatized by a divorce.

When she tried to coax Robert into therapy, he resisted steadfastly. She considered threatening a divorce but knew she could never make good on the threat; the children were too young and she loved them too much to put them through that. Finally, knowing that Robert loved the children as much as she did even though he spent little time with them, Lynn approached him not on her own behalf, but on theirs. She told him that they needed a father who could give them emotional support, that he needed to start closing the gap between him and his children or they would never be close again. She didn't even mention her own needs. Although he continued to resist the need for professional help, he did agree to "sit in" on an informal church-sponsored encounter group for couples.

In the first two sessions, Robert was distant and suspicious. Then, in the third session, the moderator asked Lynn to talk about her husband. She stood up and faced him. She was still the most elegant, most graceful woman he had ever known, and all he could think when she turned toward him was "I don't deserve it." He had never felt more inadequate in his life, and the realization that she was slipping away stung him deeply.

Lynn spoke softly, and her eyes never left him. "I love my husband," she began. "He means more to me than anything in life." She went on to talk about how smart he was, how hard he worked. She told them that he was a great doctor and she was proud to be his wife. She told them about his parents: about his father, the policeman, who was so proud of his son that he carried a picture of Robert on his graduation day in his wallet and showed it to shopkeepers on his beat; about his mother, who boasted that she had to make enough dough for ten thousand rolls to pay for one day of her son's education—and she would do it all her life to see her son a doctor. "I love them," she said. "And I love the part of them that's in my husband."

She told them that she was there because she wanted to help their marriage; that she wished he could feel comfortable enough around her to open up to her, to share his problems, his doubts, his insecurities, to tell her his problems from time to time, to let down the facade and let her love *him,* not the man he thought he had to be to deserve her love.

Robert was moved. For the first time, he realized that she loved him *and* respected him—that he didn't need to pretend anymore. There were no overnight miracles, of course. But Robert agreed to start seeing a therapist regularly. That was a major victory. "With time," Lynn told us, "things between us have become so much easier. He talks more easily. I really feel like I'm sharing his life again. He's so much more open and relaxed now that he doesn't feel under constant pressure to impress the world—or me."

A Guide to Therapy

Although most men, like Robert, need help to overcome their insecurities, few are willing to ask for it, or even accept its offer. If the help comes in the form of professional therapy, the fear of disclosure can be especially strong and stubborn. Therefore, it's usually the woman who, like Lynn, must assume the burden of arranging appropriate therapy and convincing the man of the need for it. This brief guide is for women who face those challenges. It's only a beginning, of course, but in therapy, the first step is always the hardest.

Who Should Seek Professional Help? Virtually all of the psychologists and psychiatrists we spoke with recommended outside help for men who can't overcome a fear of dependence. But few were very enthusiastic about the universal benefits of protracted individual analysis or therapy; the consensus was that a man should be encouraged to see an analyst or therapist only if his problems are very serious. No solution is to be discarded, and more than one solution may be appropriate. But most experts recommend that a couple who want outside help consider marital counseling.

"Therapy," said a New York psychiatrist, "is on the heavy end of things. Instead of individual therapy, I'd recommend a marriage encounter group, the kind in which people get together and focus on such topics as sex in marriage, what you do when your children grow up, and the pitfalls in going back and having a career." All couples need to air the problems in their relationship from time to time. A marriage encounter group can offer couples who have stopped communicating a comfortable setting for discussing those issues again.

When Is Marital Therapy Needed? Marital therapy may not be as expensive, time-consuming, or threatening as individual analysis, but it's still a major step—not necessarily the solution for every man who has trouble expressing his emotions or every woman who wants to help a man be more expressive. We asked Dr. Hal Arkowitz, professor of psychology at Arizona State University and a practicing therapist, how a man and woman can tell if they should seek professional assistance.

"If one partner or the other wonders whether the couple needs professional help," Dr. Arkowitz told us, "they should set up a one-shot meeting with a professional." More likely than not, only one of the partners—generally the woman—is actively concerned about the problem, and she may have to visit the therapist on her own. But it is certainly preferable if she lets her partner know that she wants to seek professional assistance and if she asks her partner to participate. "This initial meeting," Arkowitz adds, "is comparable to a physical checkup. Say to the therapist, 'Here are our concerns. Do you really think we need help? Or is it something we can work out on our own?' "

It's rare for a couple to seek marital counseling unless they are facing a crisis. "Usually, there has to be a crisis for people to want to learn new ways," says marital therapist Marcha Ortiz. "There's still a stigma to getting any kind of help. People often don't come for help unless there is a driving force, and often this driving force is a problem with the children: the children are in trouble at school, or with the police, or they're in trouble with alcohol. Or maybe one of the parents is having an affair, or is an alcoholic, or something has happened to disturb the balance of the relationship. Very few people come in voluntarily for help."

Getting Him into Therapy. Many men will avoid seeking professional help if they think they are responsible for the problem. "I do a lot of marriage therapy," a psychologist in the Midwest told us. "The complaint that 'my husband doesn't open up to me' is probably one of the most common complaints I hear. But I have hardly ever encountered a man complaining that 'my wife doesn't open up to me about herself.' It's almost always the other way around. Men tend to be more amenable to the idea of therapy if they think that the problem is the woman's problem, or the child's problem —anyone other than themselves."

If a husband or lover resists professional therapy, a woman shouldn't argue that *he* needs therapy. She should tell him that *she* is having problems in the relationship and that her therapy can be successful only if he participates. "Ask him for his help," says Cese MacDonald. "Two people are involved in the relationship, and for it to improve, the help of both is needed. A woman often needs to tell her husband or lover that she is stuck without his help and that she needs him there.

"Often the resistance comes from the man's fear that the therapist will take the wife's side. In situations where the woman made the initial contact, I suggest that they see another marital counselor, someone who has never worked with either of them before, so that they can come in fresh. In other words, I make it clear that I don't care who takes care of their problems as long as somebody does."

Finding a Good Marital Therapist. In most states therapists must be licensed and certified, psychologists must have a Ph.D. and pass an exam, and psychiatrists must have an M.D., meet residency requirements, and be board-certified. In some states there are additional minimum-experience requirements. Social workers should be members of the National Academy of Social Workers, and "counselors," although not subject to any requirements, are usually certified. The appropriate state boards should be checked to ensure that a person meets the appropriate standards.

"But even if you check all the right associations," Arkowitz says, "you can still run into some absolute dodos who are beautifully certified and trained in some of the best places in the world whom I wouldn't recommend to an enemy. Not that they aren't ethical, just that they aren't any good at therapy, which is both a talent and a science."

Arkowitz suggests looking for experience as well as training. He recommends choosing a senior therapist who has lived in the community for a long time over a less experienced but better-credentialed one. "Try to get an impartial assessment," he says, "by asking a professor of psychology at a local university or someone in a related field. Narrow the candidates to two or three and then set up a meeting with each. The interview process can be emotionally exhausting, because you're telling your whole story to two or three different people. But your time, your money, and your relationship are on the line. You'll be glad you were choosy. Most therapists don't charge for a consultation."

Another possible source of counseling is a marital group run free of charge by a community or church. The usefulness of such groups, however, depends entirely on the quality of those who run them. People who have already participated in a marital program are the best source of information on its effectiveness. In almost any community there is likely to be at least one group that can help a couple work out problems in a relationship that are too difficult for them to work out by themselves.

The Price of Doing Without

The final argument for therapy is what happens when a man does without it. "Sometimes the best way to convince a man that he needs help is to tie it to his health," says a New York psychoanalyst. "It may not be enough to say, 'Your mental health is threatened.' Many people don't think that psychological damage is damage at all. But if you tell him what not being able to express his emotions can do to his body, you might just scare him into seeking help. With all the mania for fitness and health, the argument can be persuasive. The facts are there, and they're very scary."

The facts are these:

Men live shorter lives than women—eight years shorter, on the average. The heart-attack rate among men is seven times the rate among women. Whether death comes from heart disease, cirrhosis of the liver, pneumonia, influenza, or cancer, it comes to men more often. Of the sixty-four causes of death enumerated by the leading insurance companies, fifty-seven give men preferential treatment. And if a man is afflicted by one of the remaining seven causes, such as high blood pressure, he's more likely to die of it than is a woman. "The truth," says Dr. John H. Laragh of the New York Hospital–Cornell Medical Center, "is that men don't tolerate *anything* as well as women."

According to the U.S. Department of Labor, men are six times more likely than women to suffer death or disabling disease on the job. When they do become sick, they refuse to take care of themselves. Dr. Charles Lewis and Mary Ann Lewis reported in the *New England Journal of Medicine* that men are generally "reluctant to seek care or adopt behavior that would diminish the risks of dying sooner from chronic diseases."

In a recent study Sidney Jourard explored the significance of emotional openness—which he called "self-disclosure"—in men's lives. "To compensate for their lack of self-disclosure," he concluded, "men tend to depend in a stereotypical way on gainful employment, enviable status, and sexual potency to give meaning to their lives. Once these achievements are gone, men have no other resources, become dispirited, and are subject to an early death."

The closed man has nowhere to redirect his problems, no outlet for the stress and anxiety that inevitably accumulate inside. According to Jourard, lack of self-disclosure "produced more internalized secrets, more tension, more expenditure of energy, and more stress" than among women. "There's a lot of tension that men can never let off," says Dr. Alexander Levay, "and the psychological effects are great. They bottle it all up. The results are obvious. The statistics are there."

Within the body, the process of self-destruction takes a variety of forms. Constant stress and unrelieved tension cause the body to release fats into the bloodstream. Protective secretions in the stomach are reduced; digestive acids burn ulcers in the stomach walls. The colon goes into painful spasms. The bladder becomes more vulnerable to infection. Deposits of cholesterol accumulate in the blood vessels leading to the heart. Blood pressure goes up. The heart palpitates. Muscles in the face, neck, and scalp go into prolonged, involuntary contractions, resulting in headaches. Blood vessels supplying the brain dilate furiously, causing migraines.

Tears, the closed man's mark of shame, are being seen increasingly as important elements in maintaining emotional health. A two-year study by Dr. David Goodman in California indicates that crying can relieve cardiovascular problems— by crying more often, both men and women can reduce their blood pressure by 20 to 25 percent. Doctors at St. Joseph's College in St. Paul, Minnesota, found that tears of emotion —tears shed during a time of grief or crisis—contain toxins not found in ordinary, cleansing tears. The body produces these toxins under stress and eliminates them through the tear duct. By holding tears back during emotional or stressful periods, a man prevents his body from ridding itself of harmful chemicals. The rule that "men don't cry" means they must slowly poison themselves.

A Life Without Color

Although the arguments for emotional openness based on health are strong, the highest price men pay for their inexpressiveness doesn't lend itself to statistical analysis. Its value can be measured only in lost opportunities. A lifetime of unexpressed emotions and unshared feelings leaves a man emotionally impoverished: in Karen Horney's words, "without intensity," "dull and flattened out."

This, ultimately, is the cost of being closed. Cut off from meaningful emotional interaction with men or women, the closed man lives his life from a distance, never fully engaged in the world around him. It's as if he's reading his life in a book, instead of actually living through it himself. "Some men opt for security in lieu of feeling," says Merle Shain, "and call their decision maturity. . . . Loving can cost a lot but not loving always costs more, and those who fear to love often find that want of love is an emptiness that robs the joy from life. Men and women who don't know love often feel they've missed the essential experience of life. . . ."

When Robert and Lynn talk about the time in their relationship when they weren't communicating they sound like two people who have survived a serious illness in the family. "I look back on those years," says Robert, "and they're almost a blank, like they didn't happen." That comment brings a light, wise laugh from Lynn, as if to say, "I remember them too well." But she is clearly more concerned with the present than the past. "I look at the life we have now and all the good things in it," she says, "and then I think how we could have missed it all if we hadn't been willing to take that first step."

Out in the Open

A Personal Epilogue

HILE WORKING ON this book, trying to understand why men can't open up and how they can, we learned something about ourselves. We were forced to examine, for the first time, the roles, stereotypes, and expectations that have guided us throughout our own lives. We were confronted with all the whys that we never bothered to ask. Why are we what we are? Why do we feel (or not feel) the way we do? Why do we fear the intimacy we say we want? In short, we were forced to redefine in our own terms what it means to be a man.

Greg: Missed Opportunities. For me, this book was a trip through the past. The product of a boyhood in the Midwest—football, parties, locker rooms, and lovers' lanes—I had never thought much about what those experiences did to me, how they defined my ability to share intimacy. By tracing the development of the male role in society and seeing how that role has been played out in the lives of other men, I finally recognized how the past has controlled my relationships.

I remember vividly one particular afternoon in the

spring before work on this book began. I was in love with someone I had known almost a year, and on that afternoon in spring, I felt that love vividly. I guess it was the perfect conjunction: the time of year, the time in my life, the woman who made me smile. I sat in the kitchen of her apartment making small talk and laughing over nothing, while all the time I felt like shouting, "I love you." But she didn't hear it. Maybe I didn't hear it. The moment passed.

That was not the first or the last moment I lost to manhood. There have been many times when something inside wanted to shout but was never heard. My real feelings were seldom expressed—the hurts and the happiness. Now, looking over all those years, I feel as I did on that perfect day in spring, when I left her apartment thinking of all the things I should have said. I feel myself, in Edith Wharton's phrase, "bursting with belated eloquence."

Steve: Unanswered Questions. For me, this book has been an uncomfortable confrontation with the unanswered questions in my own life. When friendships seemed difficult, why was I so quick to bury myself in work? Why was I afraid of the effort, the frustration, and the heartache of making a relationship work? When love was what I needed most, why did I merely set new goals to achieve? Why, in times of emotional need, was I without a friend or reluctant to accept the consolation of those who called me friend? Why was I so quick to turn and run when relationships began to make emotional demands?

It's difficult to explain the process of awakening, or "rediscovering one's real self" (as Horney puts it), even in our own lives. Explaining it in a way that resonates in other men's lives is a daunting task, a task made even more frustrating by the thicket of psychological jargon and consciousness-raising cant that surrounds it. It's almost impossible to discuss the subject without sounding glib and facile. Self-realization is not a territory in which most men, especially closed men, tread confidently.

For the closed man, fact-loving and goal-oriented, the wispy jargon of self-actualization seems frivolous and self-indulgent. But rediscovering the "real self" doesn't have to be either frivolous or self-indulgent. It doesn't necessarily require prolonged analysis, group encounters, or writhing on the floor. It requires only that a man learn how he feels—not an easy task after a lifetime of learning how he should feel.

For us, discovering the "real self"—in terms even the closed man can understand—has been a matter of lifting the burden of *shoulds:* acknowledging that we feel uncertain and anxious when we *should* feel directed; admitting that we feel lonely and long for the support of friends when we *should* feel competitive; listening to the small boy inside who wants to cut up when we *should* be in control; confessing the need for others when we *should* be independent. It's a matter of being what we are rather than what we think we should be.

Ron plays professional football. He has always been as taut as a guy wire. He turns to recreation occasionally but never really relaxes; he's an incurable overachiever. Because he's nearing the end of his ball-playing career, he feels financial pressure. On the football field, he still feels the pressure to win from his teammates, and recently there has been emotional pressure at home from his girlfriend, who's impatient for marriage. Talking with him is like trying to untie a knot.

We asked him if he ever relaxed. Was he ever free of the anxiety coiled up inside him? He thought for a moment, then finally said yes—but *only* for those few brief minutes after orgasm. For those precious moments, he didn't feel the burdens. That feeling of release, of being relieved—even temporarily—of the burdens of manhood, that feeling not unlike the total reprieve of orgasm, is what the closed man feels when he finally makes contact with his real self. Release, relief, reprieve—this is a definition of openness that a man can understand.

The first step away from the fear of intimacy toward

that feeling of openness and freedom is to recognize that we need other people. The closed man's cosmology is based on the proposition that a man is—and should be—ultimately alone; that he should be able to face the world without support, without dependency, without love to lean on. Despite the contrary exhortations of literature, despite common sense, despite the anger, pleading, and tears of those who love them, many men have tried, and are still trying, to live their lives according to that unspoken assumption. Like Melville's Ahab, they are driven on "against all natural lovings and longings" into the teeth of an unfeeling world.

For many of us, the realization comes belatedly that the only real order or meaning possible in life is the order and meaning of relationships. Only a small few will win Nobel prizes, make scientific breakthroughs, write great literature, create great works of art, set records, or in some other way cheat mortality. And in these uncertain economic times, fewer and fewer of us will experience even the modest materialistic fulfillment that can hedge emotional emptiness.

For the vast majority of us, the sum total of life will be the people we have known and, more particularly, the people we have loved. Not to be loved is tragic, but not to love is catastrophic. For anyone, man or woman, to miss the opportunity to love, to go through life confined by stereotypes, prevented from sharing genuine intimacy by inherited roles and nameless fears, is, ultimately, to miss life's greatest joy and only enduring reward.

Bibliography

Adler, A. 1927. *Understanding Human Nature.* New York: Greenberg.

Adorno, T. W.; Frenkel-Brunswick, E.; Levinson, D. J.; and Sanford, R. N. 1950. *The Authoritarian Personality.* New York: John Wiley & Sons.

Allen, D. 1954. "Antifemininity in Men." *American Sociological Review* 19:581–593.

Allen, J., and Hacoun, D. 1976. "Sex Differences in Emotionality: A Multidimensional Approach. *Human Relations* 29:711–722.

Andrews, A. 1982. "The New Closeness Between Men and Women." *Self* 4 (July):53–54.

Arkowitz, H. 1977. "Measurement and Modification of Minimal Dating Behavior." *Progress in Behavior Modification* 5:1–61.

Arkowitz, H.; Lichtenstein, E.; McGovern, K.; and Hines, P. 1975. "The Behavioral Assessment of Social Competence in Males." *Behavior Therapy* 6:3–13.

Bach, G. R., and Deutsch, R. M. *Pairing: How to Achieve Genuine Intimacy.* New York: Peter H. Wyden.

Bach, G. R., and Goldberg, H. *Creative Aggression: The Art of Assertive Living.* New York: Doubleday.

Bach, G. R., and Wyden, P. 1968. *The Intimate Enemy: How to Fight Fair in Love and Marriage.* New York: William Morrow.

Balkwell, C.; Balswick, J.; and Balkwell, J. 1978. *Journal of Marriage and the Family* (November):743–747.

Balswick, J. 1979. "The Inexpressive Male: Functional-Conflict and Role Theory as Contrasting Explanations." *The Family Coordinator* (July):331–336.

Balswick, J., and Avertt, C. P. 1977. "Differences in Expressiveness: Gender, Interpersonal Orientation, and Perceived Parental Expressiveness as Contributing Factors." *Journal of Marriage and the Family* 39:121–128.

Balswick, J. O., and Balkwell, J. W. 1978. "Religious Orthodox and Emotionality." *Review of Religious Research* 19 (3):308–319.

Balswick, J. O., and Peek, C. 1971. "The Inexpressive Male: A Tragedy of American Society?" *The Family Coordinator* 20:363–368.

Barbach, L. G. 1975. *For Yourself: The Fulfillment of Female Sexuality.* New York: Doubleday.

Barbach, L. G., and Levine, L. 1980. *Shared Intimacies: Women's Sexual Experiences.* New York: Doubleday.

Bass, B. M.; Krussell, J.; and Alexander, R. 1971. "Male Managers' Attitudes Toward Working Women." *American Behavioral Scientist* 15:221–236.

Beach, F. A., ed. 1977. *Human Sexuality in Four Perspectives.* Baltimore, MD: The Johns Hopkins University Press.

Begley, M., with Carey, J. 1982. "A Healthy Dose of Laughter." *Newsweek* 100 (October 4):74.

Bell, D. H. 1982. *Being a Man: The Paradox of Masculinity.* Brattleboro, VT: The Lewis Publishing Company.

Bem, S.; Martyna, W.; and Watson, C. 1976. "Sex Typing and Androgyny: Further Explorations of the Expressive Domain." *Journal of Personality and Social Psychology* 34:1,016–1,023.

Benton, R. G., and Doehne, G. 1982. *Emotional Intimacy: The Missing Ingredient in Your Life.* New York: A & W.

Berman, P. 1981. "Are Women More Responsive than Men to the Young? A Review of Developmental and Situational Variables." *Psychological Bulletin* 88:668–695.

Berne, E. 1964. *Games People Play: The Psychology of Human Relationships.* New York: Grove Press.

————. 1970. *Sex in Human Loving.* New York: Simon and Schuster.

Berne, E.; Steiner, C.; and Kerr, C., eds. 1976. *Beyond Games and Scripts.* New York: Grove Press.

Bernikow, L. 1982. "Alone." *New York Times Magazine* (August 15):24ff.

Biller, H. 1970. "Father Absence and the Personality Development of the Young Child." *Developmental Psychology* 2:181–201.

Biller, H., and Borstelmann, L. 1967. "Masculine Development: An Integrative Review." *Merrill-Palmer Quarterly* 13:253–294.

Block, J. 1973. "Conceptions of Sex Role: Some Cross-cultural and Longitudinal Perspectives." *American Psychologist* 28:512–526.

Boehm, F. 1932. "The Femininity-Complex in Men." *International Journal of Psychoanalysis* 11:444–469.

Botwin, C., with Fine, J. L. 1979. *The Love Crisis: Hit-and-run Lovers, Jugglers, Sexual Stingies, Unreliables, Kinkies, and Other Typical Men Today.* New York: Doubleday.

Bowman, G. W.; Worthy, N. B.; and Greyser, S. A. 1965. "Are Women Executives People?" *Harvard Business Review* 43 (4):14ff.

Brandon, N. 1980. *The Psychology of Romantic Love.* Los Angeles: J. P. Tarcher.

Brothers, J. 1981. *What Every Woman Should Know About Men.* New York: Simon and Schuster.

Browmiller, S. 1975. *Against Our Will: Men, Women, and Rape.* New York: Simon and Schuster.

Burton, R., and Whiting, J. 1961. "The Absent Father and Cross-Sex Identity." *Merrill-Palmer Quarterly* 7:85–95.

Cantwell, M. 1982. "Verbal Promiscuity." *Vogue* 172 (September):342ff.

Carmichael, C. 1977. *Non-sexist Childraising.* Boston: Beacon Press.

Castleman, M. 1980. "4 Intimacies Men Don't Share with Women." *Self* 2 (December):94ff.

Cicone, M., and Ruble, D. 1978. "Beliefs About Males." *Journal of Social Issues* 34 (1):5–16.

Clark, J. V., and Arkowitz, H. 1975. "Social Anxiety and Self-evaluation of Interpersonal Performance." *Psychological Reports* 36:211–221.

Cottin Pogrebin, L. 1980. *Growing Up Free: Raising Your Child in the 80's.* New York: McGraw-Hill.

———. 1981*a.* "Alan Alda Talks About Love, Friends, Sex, Envy, Food, and a Few Not-So-Deadly Sins." *Ms* 9 (June):46ff.

———. 1981*b.* "How to Talk While Eating: The Family Dinnertime." *Ms* 10 (November):12ff.

———. 1981*c.* "One Step Forward." *Ms* 9 (April):99.

———. 1982*a.* "Are Men Discovering the Joys of Fatherhood?" *Ms* 10 (February):41ff.

———. 1982*b.* "The Selling of the Nurturing Father." *Ms* 10 (February):102.

Cox, C. 1982. "Tuning In: The Art of Good Listening." *Cosmopolitan* 192 (April):146ff.

David, D., and Branon, R., eds. 1976. *The Forty-Nine Percent Majority: The Male Sex Role.* Reading, MA: Addison-Wesley.

Day, I. 1980. "What Makes You Cry." *Ms* 8 (June):46ff.

Derlega, V., and Chaikin, A. 1976. "Norms Affecting Self-disclosure in Men and Women." *Journal of Consulting and Clinical Psychology* 44:376–380.

Deutsch, C., and Gilbert, L. 1976. "Sex Role Stereotypes: Effects on Perceptions of Self and Others and on Personal Adjustment. *A Journal of Counseling Psychology* 23:373–379.

Dew, R. F. 1982. "People Shells: How to Crack Them to Let Love In." *Self* 4 (May):56ff.

DeWolf, R. 1983. *How to Raise Your Man: The Problems of a New Style Woman in Love with an Old Style Man.* New York: Franklin Watts.

Dohan, M. H. 1983. "The Gender Gap." Ambassador (February):60ff.

Douglas, A. 1977. *The Feminization of American Culture.* New York: Alfred A. Knopf.

Douvan, E., and Adelson, J. 1968. *The Adolescent Experience.* New York: John Wiley & Sons.

Dowling, C. 1981. *The Cinderella Complex: Women's Hidden Fear of Independence.* New York: Summit Books.

Druley, D. 1980. "Do Touch: It's the Language of Love." *Self* 2 (September):72ff.

Druley, D. 1981. "Cuddler's Guide to Love." *Self* 3 (May):96ff.

Dubbert, J. 1979. *A Man's Place: Masculinity in Transition.* Englewood Cliffs, NJ: Prentice-Hall.

Ehrenreich, R. 1981. "The Politics of Talking—in Couples: Conversus Interruptus and Other Disorders. *Ms* 9 (May):46ff.

Eitzen, D. S. 1980. *Social Problems.* Boston: Allyn & Bacon.

Ellis, A. 1976. *Sex and the Liberated Man.* Secaucus, NJ: Lyle Stuart.

————. 1979. *The Intelligent Woman's Guide to Dating and Mating.* Secaucus, NJ: Lyle Stuart.

Ellis, A., and Harper, R. A. 1961*a*. *Creative Marriage.* New York: Lyle Stuart.

————. 1961*b*. *A New Guide to Rational Living.* Englewood Cliffs, NJ: Prentice-Hall.

Ellis, L. J., and Bentler, P. M. 1973. Traditional Sex-Determined Role Standards and Sex Stereotypes." *Journal of Personality and Social Psychology* 25:28–34.

Ember, C. 1978. "Men's Fear of Sex with Women: A Cross-cultural Study." *Sex Roles* 4:657–678.

Engel, E. 1982. "Of Male Bondage." *Newsweek* 99 (June 21):13.

Erikson, E. H. 1963. *Childhood and Society.* 2d ed. New York: W. W. Norton.

Farrell, W. 1975. *The Liberated Man: Beyond Masculinity: Freeing Men and Their Relationships with Women.* New York: Random House.

Fasteau, M. F. 1975. *The Male Machine.* New York: McGraw-Hill.

Feirstein, B. 1982. *Real Men Don't Eat Quiche.* New York: Pocket Books.

Fenichel, O. 1943. *The Psychoanalytic Theory of Neurosis.* New York: W. W. Norton.

Filene, P. 1975. *Him/Her/Self: Sex Roles in Modern America.* New York: Harcourt Brace.

Fisher, S., and Fisher, R. 1976. *What We Really Know About Childrearing.* New York: Simon and Schuster.

Flowers, C. E., and Abrams, M. 1980. "Sexuality: A Guide to Total Understanding." *Cosmopolitan* 188 (March):227ff.

Forisha, B. L. 1978. *Sex Roles and Personal Awareness*. Morristown, NJ: General Learning Press.

Forisha, B., and Goldman, B., eds. 1981. *Outsiders on the Inside: Women in Organizations*. Englewood Cliffs, NJ: Prentice-Hall.

Frank, E., and Enos, S. F. 1983. "The Lovelife of the American Wife." *Ladies' Home Journal* C (February):71ff.

Franks, V., and Rothblum, E. D., eds. 1983. *The Stereotyping of Women: Its Effects on Mental Health*. New York: Springer.

Friedan, B. 1963. *The Feminine Mystique*. New York: W. W. Norton.

————. 1981. *The Second Stage*. New York: Summit Books.

Friday, N. 1980. *Men in Love: Men's Sexual Fantasies: The Triumph of Love Over Rage*. New York: Delacorte Press.

Gilbert, L.; Deutsch, C.; and Strahan, R. 1978. "Feminine and Masculine Dimensions of the Typical, Desirable, and Ideal Woman and Man." *Sex Roles* 4:767–778.

Gilligan, C. 1982. *In a Different Voice: Psychological Theory and Women's Development*. Cambridge, MA: Harvard University Press.

Goldberg, H. 1976. *The Hazards of Being Male: Surviving the Myth of Masculine Privilege*. New York: Sanford J. Greenburger Associates.

————. 1979. *The New Male: From Self-Destruction to Self-Care*. New York: William Morrow.

————. 1983. *The New Male Female Relationship*. New York: William Morrow.

Gornick, V., and Moran, B. K., eds. 1971. *Woman in Sexist Society*. New York: Basic Books.

Gottlieb, A. 1983. " 'Problem? What problem?' How to Get Him to Talk About Your Marriage." *McCall's* 110 (April):14ff.

Greenberg, M., and Morris, N. 1974. "Engrossment: The Newborn's Impact upon the Father." *American Journal of Orthopsychiatry* 44:520–531.

Hall, M., and Keith, R. 1964. "Sex-role Preference Among Children of Upper- and Lower-Class." *Journal of Social Psychology* 62:101–110.

Harford, T.; Willis, C.; and Deabler, H. 1967. "Personality Correlates of Masculinity-Femininity." *Psychological Reports* 21:881–884.

Harlow, R. 1951. "Masculine Inadequacy and the Compensatory Development of Physique." *Journal of Personality* 19:312–333.

Harrison, J. 1978. "Warning: The Male Sex Role May Be Hazardous to Your Health." *Journal of Social Issues* 34 (1):65–86.

Hartley, R. L. 1959. "Sex Role Pressures in the Socialization of the Male Child." *Psychological Reports* 5:459–468.

Herman, J., and Gyllstrom, K. 1977. "Working Men and Women: Inter- and Intra-Role Conflict." *Psychology of Women Quarterly* 1:319–333.

Hershey, M. 1978. "Racial Differences in Sex-role Identities and Sex Stereotyping: Evidence Against a Common Assumption." *Social Science Quarterly* 58:584–596.

Hite, S. 1976. *The Hite Report: A Nationwide Study of Female Sexuality.* New York: Macmillan.

———. 1981. *The Hite Report on Male Sexuality.* New York: Alfred A. Knopf.

Hoffman, M. 1977. "Sex Differences in Empathy and Related Behaviors." *Psychological Bulletin* 84:712–722.

Hoffman, M. L., and Hoffman, L. W., eds. 1964. *Review of Child Development Research,* vol. 1. New York: Russell Sage Foundation.

Horney, K. 1932. "The Dread of Women." *International Journal of Psychoanalysis* 13:348–360.

———. 1937. *The Neurotic Personality of Our Time.* New York: W. W. Norton.

———. 1950. *Neurosis and Human Growth: The Struggle Toward Self-Realization.* New York: W. W. Norton.

Horney, K., and Kelman, H., eds. 1967. *Feminine Psychology.* New York: W. W. Norton.

Hunt, M. 1982. "Male/Female Brains." *Self* 4 (March):57–58.

Hyatt, I. R. 1977. *Before You Love Again.* New York: Random House.

J. 1969. *The Sensuous Woman.* Secaucus, NJ: Lyle Stuart.

Johnson, J. 1983. *Minor Characters.* Boston: Houghton Mifflin.

Jourard, S. 1964. *The Transparent Self: Self-Disclosure and Well-Being.* Princeton, NJ: Van Nostrand.

Kagan, J., and Moss, H. 1962. *Birth to Maturity: A Study in Psychological Development* 35:1051–1056.

Keller, G. D., 1977. *The Significance and Impact of Gregorio Maranon: Literary Criticism, Biographies, and Historiography.* New York: Bilingual Press/Editorial Bilingue.

Kelly, J., and Worrell, J. 1977. "New Formulations of Sex Roles and Androgyny: A Critical Review." *Journal of Consulting and Clinical Psychology* 45:1101–1115.

Kiev, A. 1979. *Active Loving: Discovering and Developing the Power to Love.* New York: Thomas Y. Crowell.

———. 1982. *How to Keep Love Alive.* New York: Harper & Row.

Kimura, D. 1973. "The Asymmetry of the Human Brain." *Scientific American* 228 (3):70–78.

———. 1983. "Sex Differences in Cerebral Organization for Speech and Praxic Functions." *Canadian Journal of Psychology* 37 (1):19–35.

Kinsey, A.; Pomeroy, W.; and Martin, C. 1948. *Sexual Behavior in the Human Male*. Philadelphia: Saunders.

Kinsey, A.; Pomeroy, W.; Martin, C.; and Gebhard, P. 1953. *Sexual Behavior in the Human Female*. Philadelphia: Saunders.

Kitagawa, E., and Hauser, P. 1973. *Differential Mortality in the United States: A Study in Socioeconomic Epidemiology*. Cambridge, MA: Harvard University Press.

Komarovsky, M. 1946. "Cultural Contradictions and Sex Roles." *American Journal of Sociology* 52:182–189.

——. 1953. *Women in the Modern World: Their Education and Their Dilemmas*. Boston: Little, Brown.

——. 1964. *Blue Collar Marriage*. New York: The Vintage Press.

——. 1975. *Dilemmas of Masculinity: A Study of College Youth*. New York: W. W. Norton.

Korda, M. 1974. *Male Chauvinism!* New York: Random House.

——. 1981. "Intimacy: Why It's so Crucial Today." *Self* 3 (February):51–55.

——. 1982. "Tenderness: How to Touch a Man's Hidden Love Nerves." *Self* 4 (February):64–67.

Koslow, S. P. 1983. "The Can't Live with Him/Can't Live Without Him Marriage." *Ladies' Home Journal* C(April):64ff.

Kosner, A. 1982. "An Intimate Chat with a Sex Therapist." *Cosmopolitan* 192 (February):202ff.

Kovel, J. 1976. *A Complete Guide to Therapy: From Psychoanalysis to Behavior Modification*. New York: Pantheon Books.

Kramer, R. 1983. *In Defense of the Family: Raising Children in America Today*. New York: Basic Books.

L'Abate, L. 1980. "Inexpressive Males or Overexpressive Females? A Reply to Balswick." *Family Relations* 29:229–230.

Lague, L. 1982. "I Love to See a Grown Man Cry." *Glamour* 80 (December):202.

Leavenworth, C. 1981. *Love & Commitment: You Don't Have to Settle for Less.* Englewood Cliffs, NJ: Prentice-Hall.

Lederer, W. 1968. *The Fear of Women*. New York: Grune and Stratton.

Levine, S., ed. 1972. *Hormones and Behavior*. New York: Academic Press.

Lewis, R. A. 1978. "Emotional Intimacy Among Men." *Journal of Social Issues* 43 (1):108–121.

Lewis, R. A., and Pleck, J. H., eds. 1979. "Men's Roles in the Family." *The Family Coordinator* 28 (4):429–626.

Lifton, R., ed. 1964. *The Woman in America*. Boston: Beacon Press.

Lorenz, K. 1963. *On Aggression.* Translated by M. K. Wilson. New York: Harcourt, Brace & World.

Love, J. 1980. "Clint Eastwood: A Sexy Legend at Fifty." *Cosmopolitan* 189 (July):182ff.

Lynn, D. B. 1966. "The Process of Learning Parental and Sex-role Identification." *Journal of Marriage and the Family* 28:466–470.

Lynn, D. B. 1969. *Parental and Sex Role Identification: A Theoretical Formulation.* Berkeley, CA: McCutchan.

M. 1971. *The Sensuous Man.* Secaucus, NJ: Lyle Stuart.

Maccoby, E. E., and Jacklin, C. N. 1974. *The Psychology of Sex Differences.* Stanford, CA: Stanford University Press.

Machlowitz, M. 1980. *Workaholics: Living with Them, Working with Them.* Reading, MA; Addison-Wesley.

Masih, L. 1967. "Career Saliency and Its Relation to Certain Needs, Interests, and Job Values." *Personal and Guidance Journal* 45:653–658.

Masters, W. H, and Johnson, V. E. 1966. *Human Sexual Response.* Boston: Little, Brown.

———. 1970. *Human Sexual Inadequacy.* Boston: Little, Brown.

May, R. 1969. *Love and Will.* New York: W. W. Norton.

———. *Freedom and Destiny.* New York: W. W. Norton.

McArthur, L., and Eisen, S. 1976*a.* "Achievement of Male and Female Storybook Characters as Determinants of Achievement Behavior by Boys and Girls." *Journal of Personality and Social Psychology* 33:467–473.

———. 1976*b.* "Television and Sex-role Stereotyping." *Journal of Applied Social Psychology* 6:329–351.

McGinnis, L. 1980. "What to Do when Your Man Won't Talk." *Cosmopolitan* 188 (March):164ff.

Mead, M. 1935. *Sex and Temperament in Three Primitive Societies.* New York: William Morrow.

———. *Male & Female: A Study of the Sexes in a Changing World.* New York: William Morrow.

Mellen, J. 1978. *Big Bad Wolves: Masculinity in the American Film.* New York: Pantheon Books.

Meyer-Bahlburg, H. F. L.; Boon, D.; Sharma, M.; and Edwards, J. 1974. "Aggressiveness and Testosterone Measures in Man." *Psychosomatic Medicine* 36:269–274.

Michaels, L. 1981. *The Men's Club.* New York: Farrar Straus Giroux.

Miller, D., and Swanson, G. 1960. *Inner Conflict and Defense.* New York: Holt, Rinehart & Winston.

Miller, S. *Men and Friendship.* Boston: Houghton Mifflin.

Mitchell, G.; Redican, W.; and Gomber, J. 1974. "Lessons from a Primate: Males Can Raise Babies." *Psychology Today* (April):23–28.

Money, J., and Ehrhardt, A. 1972. *Man and Woman, Boy and Girl.* Baltimore, MD: Johns Hopkins University Press.

Morgenstern, M., with Naifeh, S., and Smith, G. W. 1982. *How to Make Love to a Woman.* New York: Clarkson N. Potter.

Mussen, P. 1961. "Some Antecedents and Consequents of Masculine Sex-typing in Adolescent Boys." *Psychological Monographs* 75 (2):1–24.

Mussen, P. 1962. "Long-term Consequents of Masculinity Interests in Adolescence." *Journal of Consulting Psychology* 26:435–440.

Mussen, P., and Rutherford, E. 1963. "Parent-Child Relations and Parental Personality in Relation to Young Children's Sex-role Preferences." *Child Development* 34:589–607.

Novak, W. 1983. *The Great American Man Shortage.* New York: Rawson Associates.

Olsen, P. 1981. *Sons and Mothers: Why Men Behave as They Do.* New York: M. Evans.

Parke, R. D. 1981. *Fathers.* Cambridge, MA: Harvard University Press.

Peck, M. S. 1978. *The Road Less Traveled: A New Psychology of Love, Traditional Values and Spiritual Growth.* New York: A Touchstone Book.

Penny, A. 1981. *How to Make Love to a Man.* New York: Clarkson N. Potter.

Persky, H.; Smith, K. D.; and Basu, G. R. 1971. "Relations of Psychological Measures of Aggression and Hostility to Testosterone Production in Men." *Psychosomatic Medicine* 33:265–277.

Petras, J. W. 1975. *Sex: Male/Gender: Masculine: Readings in Male Sexuality.* Port Washington, NY: Alfred.

Pietropinto, A., and Simenauer, J. 1977. *Beyond the Male Myth: What Women Want to Know About Men's Sexuality.* New York: Quadrangle.

———. 1979. *Husbands and Wives.* New York: Times Books.

Pleck, J. H. 1975. "Masculinity-Femininity: Current and Alternate Paradigms." *Sex Roles* 1:161–178.

———. 1976. "The Male Sex Role: Definitions, Problems, and Sources of Change." *Journal of Social Issues* 32 (3):155–164.

———. 1978. "Men's Traditional Attitudes Toward Women: Correlates of Adjustment or Maladjustment?" *Psychological Reports* 42:975–983.

———. 1981. *The Myth of Masculinity.* Cambridge, MA: The MIT Press.

Pleck, J. H., and Brannon, R., eds. 1978. "Male Roles and the Male Experience. *Journal of Social Issues* 34 (1):1–199.

Pleck, J. H., and Sawyer, J. 1974. *Men and Masculinity.* Englewood Cliffs, NJ: Prentice-Hall.

Plog, S. 1965. "The Disclosure of Self in the United States and Germany." *Journal of Social Psychology* 65:193–203.

Rich, A. 1976. *Of Woman Born*. New York: W. W. Norton.

Ricker, A. L. 1980. "Sex for Sale in Las Vegas." *Cosmopolitan* 189 (November): 280ff.

Riesman, D., with Glazer, N., and Denney, R. 1950. *The Lonely Crowd: A Study of the Changing American Character*. New Haven, CT: Yale University Press.

Rodriguez, R. 1983. *Hunger of Memory*. New York: Bantam Books.

Rosaldo, M. S., and Lamphere, L., eds. 1974. *Woman, Culture, and Society*. Stanford, CA: Stanford University Press.

Rose, F., and Bennett, G. 1980. *Real Men: Sex and Style in an Uncertain Age*. New York: Doubleday.

Rosenberg, B., and Sutton-Smith, B. 1960. "A Revised Conception of Masculine-Feminine Differences in Play Activities." *Journal of Genetic Psychology* 96:165–170.

Ross, D., and Ross, S. 1972. "Resistance by Preschool Boys to Sex-Inappropriate Behavior." *Journal of Educational Psychology* 63:342–346.

Ross, E. 1981. "Still Needed: A New Look at an Old Institution." *Ms* 9 (March):52.

Rothbart, M. K., and Maccoby, E. E. 1966. "Parents' Differential Reactions to Sons and Daughters." *Journal of Personality and Social Psychology* 4:237–243.

Rubin, L. 1983. *Intimate Strangers*. New York: Harper & Row.

Rubin, T. I. 1980. *Reconciliations: Inner Peace in an Age of Anxiety*. New York: The Viking Press.

Rubin, T. I., and Berliner, D. C. 1977. *Understanding Your Man: A Woman's Guide*. New York: Ballantine Books.

Rudy, A. J., and Peller, R. 1972. "Men's Liberation." *Medical Aspects of Human Sexuality* 6 (September):84–85.

Sager, C. J., and Hunt, B. 1979. *Intimate Partners: Hidden Patterns in Love Relationships*. New York: McGraw-Hill.

Savan, L. 1981. "Learning Not to Confess." *Cosmopolitan* 191 (August):168ff.

Schaffer, R. 1977. *Mothering*. Cambridge, MA: Harvard University Press.

Scott, J. P., and Scott, S. F., eds. 1971. *Social Control and Social Change*. Chicago: University of Chicago Press.

Sennett, R., and Cobb, J. 1972. *The Hidden Injuries of Class*. New York: Random House.

Seward, G., and Williamson, R., eds. 1970. *Sex Roles in Changing Society*. New York: Random House.

Sexton, P. C. 1970. *The Feminized Male: Classrooms, White Collars, and the Decline of Maleness*. New York: Vintage Books.

Shain, M. 1976. *Some Men Are More Perfect than Others*. New York: Bantam.

———. 1978. *When Lovers Are Friends*. Philadelphia: J. B. Lippincott.

Sheehy, G. 1976. *Passages: Predictable Crises of Adult Life*. New York: E. P. Dutton.

———. 1981. *Pathfinders*. New York: William Morrow.

Silvern, L. 1977. "Children's Sex-role Preferences: Stronger Among Girls than Boys." *Sex Roles* 3:159–171.

Skjei, E., and Rabkin, R. 1981. *The Male Ordeal: Role Crisis in a Changing World*. New York: G. P. Putnam's Sons.

Solomon, R. C. 1981. *Love: Emotion, Myth and Metaphor*. New York: Anchor Press/Doubleday.

Spence, J. T., and Helmreich, R. L. 1978. *Masculinity & Femininity: Their Psychological Dimensions, Correlates, and Antecedents*. Austin, TX: University of Texas Press.

———. 1979. "On Assessing 'Androgyny.' " *Sex Roles* 5:721–738.

Staples, R., ed. 1971*a*. *The Black Family: Essays and Studies*. Belmont, CA: Brooks/Cole.

———. 1971*b*. "The Myth of the Impotent Black Male." *Black Scholar* 2 (10): 2–9.

———. 1978. "Masculinity and Race: The Dual Dilemma of Black Men." *Journal of Social Issues* 34 (1):169–183.

Stearns, P. 1979. *Be a Man! Males in Modern Society*. New York: Holmes and Meier.

Stein, H. 1983. "Why Do Boys Have a Hard Time Expressing Their Feelings?" *Seventeen* 42 (February):101ff.

Steinem, G. 1981. "In the Middle of the Backlash: Some Cheerful Words About Men." *Ms* 9 (June):43ff.

Stern, D. 1977. *The First Relationship: Infant and Mother*. Cambridge, MA: Harvard University Press.

Stockard, J., and Johnson, M. 1979. "The Social Origins of Male Dominance." *Sex Roles* 5:199–218.

Stone, L. 1981. "Women who Live with Gay Men." *Ms* 10 (October):103ff.

Sullerot, E. 1971. *Women, Society, and Change*. New York: McGraw-Hill.

Tannen, D. 1982. "When Men and Women Talk—Why Don't We Say What We Mean?" *Vogue* 172 (October):185ff.

Tavris, C. 1977. "Masculinity." *Psychology Today* 10 (8) (January):35ff.

Tiger, L. 1969. *Men in Groups*. New York: Random House.

Toby, J. 1966. "Violence and the Masculine Mystique: Some Quantitative Data." *Annals of the American Academy of Political and Social Science* 36 (4):19–27.

Tolson, A. 1977. *The Limits of Masculinity: Male Identity and Women's Liberation*. New York: Harper & Row.

van Praag, H. H. 1980. *Handbook of Biological Psychiatry*. New York: Marcel Dekker.

Wagenvoord, J., and Bailey, P. 1978. *Men: A Book for Women*. New York: Avon.

Wakefield, J.; Sasek, J.; Friedman, A.; and Bowden, J. 1976. "Androgyny and Other Measures of Masculinity-Femininity." *Journal of Consulting and Clinical Psychology* 44:766–770.

Waldron, I. 1976. "Why Do Women Live Longer than Men?" *Journal of Human Stress* 2:1–13.

Wanderer, Z., and Fabian, E., 1979. *Making Love Work: New Techniques in the Art of Staying Together*. New York: G. P. Putnam's Sons.

Ward, W. P. 1969. "Process of Sex Role Development." *Developmental Psychology* 9:163–168.

———. 1973. "Patterns of Culturally Defined Sex-role Preference and Parental Imitation." *Journal of Genetic Psychology* 122:337–343.

Warsaw, J. L. 1981. "Sharing Intimacies Is Not Always Intimate." *Self* 3 (February):80–81.

Washburn, S. 1981. "Touchy Turf: His/Her Power Bases: How to Allow Each Other Territory." *Self* 3 (July):95ff.

Webb, A. P. 1963. "Sex-role Preferences and Adjustments in Early Adolescents." *Child Development* 34:609–618.

Weisinger, H., and Lobsenz, N. M. 1982. "Sexual Criticism: How to Give and Take It." *Cosmopolitan* 193 (July):78ff.

Weller, S. 1981*a*. "Why We Spill Our Private Selves in Public: Interview with Studs Terkel." *Self* 3 (February):78–80.

———. 1981*b*. "Keeping Private Pieces of Yourself: Interview with Kathy Cronkite." *Self* 3 (February):81–82.

Whyte, W. H. 1956. *The Organization Man*. New York: Simon and Schuster.

Wolner, T. 1980. "The Myth of the Unemotional Man." *Cosmopolitan* 188 (January): 180ff.

Woronoff, I. 1962. "Negro Male Identification Problems." *Journal of Educational Sociology* 36:30–32.

Worrell, J., and Worrell, L. 1977. "Support and Opposition to the Women's Liberation Movement: Some Personality and Parental Correlates." *Journal of Research in Personality* 11:10–20.